Understanding Development
People, Markets and the State in Mixed Economies

Understanding Development
People, Markets and the State in Mixed Economies

IGNACY SACHS

OXFORD
UNIVERSITY PRESS

OXFORD
UNIVERSITY PRESS

YMCA Library Building, Jai Singh Road, New Delhi 110001

Oxford University Press is a department of the University of Oxford. It furthers the
University's objective of excellence in research, scholarship, and education
by publishing worldwide in

Oxford   New York

Athens   Auckland   Bangkok   Bogota   Buenos Aires   Calcutta
Cape Town   Chennai   Dar es Salaam   Delhi   Florence   Hong Kong   Istanbul
Karachi   Kuala Lumpur   Madrid   Melbourne   Mexico City   Mumbai
Nairobi   Paris   Sao Paolo   Singapore   Taipei   Tokyo   Toronto   Warsaw

with associated companies in   Berlin   Ibadan

Oxford is a registered trade mark of Oxford University Press
in the UK and in certain other countries

Published in India
By Oxford University Press, New Delhi

© Oxford University Press 2000

ISBN   0 19   564898 6

Typeset in Garamond (TTF)
by Excellent Laser Typesetters, Pitampura, Delhi 110035
Printed in India at Rashtriya Printers, Delhi 110032
Published by Manzar Khan, Oxford University Press
YMCA Library Building, Jai Singh Road, New Delhi 110 001

Foreword

Ignacy Sachs, a distinguished scholar in the structuralist intellectual tradition, has made important contributions to our understanding of development. He is as much at home in France as he is in Poland and as much at home in India as he is in Brazil. For he has lived, studied and taught in these countries, to cross the divides between East and West as also North and South. This rich, almost unique, experience is reflected in his writings on development.

It is only appropriate that this book is being published in India, because Professor Sachs has been strongly influenced by its economy, polity and society in his thinking about development. And his connection with India goes back a long time. It began in 1947 as a young Sachs in distant Brazil, bored with his curriculum in philosophy, plunged into a study of Indian thought and religion inspired by Mahatma Gandhi. The shock of Gandhi's death moved Ignacy Sachs to write an obituary entitled 'Our Saint from There', which was the first publication in his life.

Sachs returned to his native Poland in 1954 to work at the Institute for International Affairs in Warsaw. But the India connection was destined. In 1957, the director of this institute was appointed Poland's ambassador to India, and Sachs joined him as secretary for scientific and technical cooperation in the embassy. On arrival, he also enrolled as a Ph.D. student at the Delhi School of Economics where he worked under the supervision of Professor B. N. Ganguli. Ignacy Sachs was the first European to receive a doctorate at the University of Delhi.

The three years from 1957 to 1960, his work on development and underdevelopment started with the discovery of India. The contact with Indian culture and ways of life, Sachs believes, taught him the relevance of socio-cultural aspects of development and aroused his suspicions about the limitations of economics. Reading

Gandhi enriched his understanding concerning the fallacy of a single concept of modernity, the importance of ethical motivations and the significance of ecological thinking. The challenge of development, it became clear, was about uplifting the masses from poverty. Observing Nehru stimulated his interest in development alternatives, as he came to recognize the pioneering nature of India's search for a middle-path that combined economic planning with political democracy.

The stay in India was more than an education, as it opened up opportunities in Poland. In the late 1950s, India was a role model and Delhi was a diplomatic capital for the world. There were many eminent personalities, in particular distinguished economists, who visited India at the time in response to an invitation from Prime Minister Nehru. Among them were the two outstanding Polish economists: Oscar Lange and Michal Kalecki. At the time, Sachs assisted Kalecki during his stay in Delhi. It was the beginning of a life long association. Ignacy Sachs adopted Michal Kalecki as his *guru*. On his return to Poland, Sachs worked closely with Kalecki at the Central School of Planning and Statistics in Warsaw from 1960 to 1968. Together, they established a Research Centre for underdeveloped countries in 1961 (Sachs became the Director while Kalecki was the Chairman) and started an advanced course in Planning for Economists from Developing Countries sponsored by the United Nations. For both, the case of India was paradigmatic in their thinking on development. And the collaboration with India continued, through research scholars and visiting lecturers alike. This phase came to an abrupt end in 1968, after the invasion of Czechoslovakia, as a result of political repression that had started even earlier. Michal Kalecki resigned. Ignacy Sachs left Poland for France, to join the Ecole des Haute Etudes in Sciences Sociales in Paris. He has stayed there ever since. The interest in India continued in Paris where Daniel and Alice Thorner were his colleagues.

In his writings, Ignacy Sachs has always emphasized that economic growth is a necessary but not a sufficient condition for economic development. Polanyi's emphasis on the need to study the interface between society and economy is, therefore, essential for understanding. For development is about the transformation of whole societies beyond enclaves. Institutions and strategies cannot be left to markets alone. Indeed, markets only function when they are properly regulated. Inspired by the work of Kalecki, Sachs seeks to focus on the political economy of development. The approach is very different from mainstream economics. For one, the primary concern is people's livelihood. For another, the primacy of political decisions is recognized.

The essays in this volume epitomize this approach. Most of them are the outcome of research which was a lead-up to, or was a follow-up of, the Earth Summit at Rio de Janeiro in 1992 and the Social Summit at Copenhagen in 1995, as the author was closely associated with both. Consequently, there are two themes that the author explores in these essays: first, environment and development and, second, throughout, is on people.

The essential message is that sustainable development in this age of liberalization and globalization calls for alternative development paradigms and strategies, so that states, markets and people in mixed economies evolve a compact on development as social partners. The author broadens the domain of his development paradigm to encompass ecology and anthropology. Critical of the neo-liberal orthodoxy, he stresses the importance of democratic regulation of mixed economies. Liberalization and globalization, he feels, must be complemented with strategic forms of state intervention to ensure that economic progress is equitable for the people and sustainable for the environment. The political economy of development is reconsidered in terms of issues such as the provision of livelihoods and jobs, the management of biodiversity, or social equity and environmental viability.

Professor Sachs argues that, at the end of the twentieth century, there is a crisis in the world economy which cannot be ignored because it affects, albeit in different forms and with unequal intensity, almost every country in the world. In the South, poverty and deprivation persist on a massive scale. In the East, the transition from planning to markets has played havoc. In the North, unemployment levels are high despite growth. Social exclusion, regional disparities and dual economies are no longer confined to the developing world but have spread everywhere. The structural transformation in the world economy is compounding these difficulties, as there is an emerging mismatch between the growth of output and the creation of employment opportunities, a weakening link between the real economy and the financial, and a widening gap between the increase in material output and the increase in the volume of raw materials required to produce it.

Economic inequalities within countries and between countries, Sachs believes, are inherent in the working of contemporary economic systems, so that the same process leads to affluence of a minority and deprivation of the majority. Environmental disruption occurs at both ends of the spectrum. The affluent minority over-consumes scarce non-renewable resources while the deprived majority over-uses life-supporting systems simply for survival. The time has come, Sachs thinks, for the whole world to ask itself Gandhi's question: 'How much is enough?' It is clear that the North cannot continue to be profligate in its consumption patterns and lifestyles which are so intensive in the use of energy and resources. It is also clear that the South should not initiate patterns of development from the industrialized world, for it can only recreate such enclaves of modernity and prosperity for a few at the expense of many. Thus, the author concludes that there is need for both the North and the South to steer newer, if not original, development paths, informed by a more egalitarian vision of society and a different hierarchy of needs.

The moral of the story outlined by Ignacy Sachs is that the environmental revolution, sometimes described as the ecologization of minds, should force us to reconceptualize development. In this endeavour, it is necessary to evolve need-oriented eco-development strategies. The object should be to ensure that the economic system produces all the goods and services required to meet the basic needs of the world population without any further environmental disruption. Such a world, in which socio-economic progress and environmental gains go together, represents a clear positive-sum game. Eco-development strategies, which are environment-friendly and people-friendly, should seek to exploit these opportunities for a win-win outcome.

New Delhi   DEEPAK NAYYAR
September 1999

Contents

Introduction

Rhetorical commitment to the idea of development has come of age during the second half of the twentieth century. It will be up to the next generation(s) to bridge the gap, as wide as ever, between words and deeds, advancing from the idea of development to political economy of development.

It is a tall order indeed, given the setback suffered over the last two decades, marked by a considerable slow-down of the world economy, going hand in hand with the explosion of financial speculation and a further worsening of disparities between the rich and the poor, among and within countries.

Massive unemployment and underemployment and the ensuing social exclusion became, once again, an almost universal phenomenon, encompassing many industrialized countries. This unexpected reunification of the development problematique—a kind of *third worldization* of the whole planet[1]—does not make any easier the plight of the victims of maldevelopment processes, be it in the South or in the North. But it underscores the centrality of the multidimensional concept of development, as distinct from, and broader than, economic growth.

Economic growth is a necessary, but by no means a sufficient condition of development predicated on the twin ethical imperatives of synchronic and diachronic solidarity with the present and the future generations.

We need an *employment-led* growth not a *jobless* one, full-employment (and/or self-employment) being more than ever the paramount development objective; a growth improving the distribution of assets and incomes, instead of further concentrating

---

[1] As observed by S. Chakravarty, theories of dualism and fragmented labour markets have moved from developing to developed countries.

them in the hands of a few—the wealth of a country cannot be measured by the number of millionaires living there; a growth refusing the immediate profit taking from predatory exploitation of the capital of nature, establishing instead an *economy of perfor-mance* in J. C. Kumarappa's terms.

The development paradigm resulting from the normative stance just outlined is clearly incompatible with the market theology and the monetarist theories, which nowadays dominate mainstream thinking, informing the action of governments and international agencies.

At the time of writing this introduction, after Mexico, Thailand, South Korea, Indonesia and Russia, Brazil became the latest, but probably not the last victims of the neoliberal policy package known as the Washington Consensus meant to transform ailing developing economies into respectable *emerging markets*, capable of attracting massive foreign investment. The International Monetary Fund, assisted by the World Bank and inspired by the American Treasury, provides the advice and the money to stabilize the battered currency, while imposing a severe conditionality: devaluation, budget austerity, outright opening of the economy, high rates of interest and privatization of public banks and enterprises to woo foreign capital. The main (if not the only) goal is to make sure that the interest of the foreign investors will be safeguarded. The resulting social cost is to be mitigated by a few emergency programmes, preferably left to the World Bank.[2]

---

[2] A recent assessment of the social impact of the financial crisis in Asia lists the following six channels through which the people are hit. 'First, unemployment is visibly rising due to business failures or retrenchment; alternatively, many firms are cutting wages, reducing employee benefits, or shortening work hours. Second, prices of imported goods or items with high import content are escalating. Third, asset values are lost owing to the collapse of stock and real estate markets, and lifetime savings are gone due to banking failures. Fourth, diminished collateral for loans along with high interest rates is constricting access to credit for investment or consumption. Fifth, government revenue is down, while a good deal of public expenditure is being diverted toward the restructuring of financial institutions and debt servicing. Finally, the demand for migrant workers throughout the region is declining, thereby hurting countries that rely on overseas labour markets for employment of their surplus labour and for worker remittances', (*Asian Development Bank Review*, vol. 30, nr. 4, 1998).

With time, the latter started to question the validity of the approach and the underlying tenets of monetary orthodoxy, in particular the devastating effects of high rates of interest on already depressed economies. In January 1998, the senior vice-president and chief economist of the Bank, Joseph E. Stiglitz, made a plea to move beyond the Washington Consensus, criticized by him for confusing means with ends and taking privatization and liberalization as ends in themselves. His views on a new paradigm for development were further elaborated and suggestively argued in the 1998 Prebisch Lecture[3] and influenced the World Bank report on global economic prospects in developing countries.[4]

For students of the first post-War generation of progressive development thinkers, Stiglitz may not be cutting new ground by saying that development is about transformation of whole societies beyond enclaves and projects, that Polanyi was right in emphasizing the need to study the interface between society and economy, that institutions, starting with the governments, are important, that development strategies cannot be left to market forces alone and that markets only function when they are properly regulated. Somewhat regrettably he stops short of advocating planning, while presenting the financial system as the *brain* of the development game. Nevertheless, the stance taken by Stiglitz marks a welcome departure from the neoliberal orthodoxy and narrow 'economicism'. What really matters is the pertinence of ideas, not their novelty, especially since it is from a World Bank executive.

The present volume of essays results from research conducted on the occasion of the Earth and Social Summits (Rio de Janeiro, 1992 and Copenhagen, 1995) and their aftermath.[5] It is predicated on the concept of *political economy of development* inspired by the

---

[3] See Stiglitz, J. E. (1998a, 1998b).

[4] See World Bank (1998).

[5] Chapters 1 and 2 were originally written as papers for the Programme MOST (Management of Social Transformations) of UNESCO. Chapters 4, 5 and 8 were presented at the Copenhagen Seminar for Social Progress in 1996, 1997 and 1998. The conclusion is adapted from a paper written in collaboration with Vasant Gowariker published in *Economic and Political Weekly*, 4 June 1994 (See Sachs, I., 1994a). The permission to use these texts in this book is gratefully acknowledged. For my earlier work on the subject, see Sachs, I. (1963, 1966, 1979, 1987 and 1993).

writings of M. Kalecki[6] and aptly analysed by S. Chakravarty,[7] very different from mainstream economics by its primary concern with people's livelihoods and the recognition of the preeminence of political decisions, the need to practise *responsible voluntarism* informed by flexible planning.

Employment and income distribution become the entry points in the strategy of development and not mere outcomes of a market-led growth. Insofar as agriculture is the main source of employment and of wage goods, peasant farming and land reforms are subjects of particular concern. Mixed economy, with different mixes of public and private sectors, is the main institutional category, the only one left after the collapse of real socialism, given the utopian character of a pure market economy.

Having been associated since 1970 with the rethinking of social sciences in the light of environmental awareness, I have tried to broaden the planner's perspective by opening it to ecology and to cultural anthropology. The environmental revolution, sometimes described as the *ecologization of mind* forced us to reconceptualize development. According to the influential report of the Dag Hammarskjöld Foundation, development ought to rest on five pillars: it ought to be *indigenous, self-reliant, need-oriented, environment friendly and open to institutional change.*[8] To achieve it, it is necessary to empower the people and recognize the third sector represented by the organized civil society as a major emerging actor on the development scene. This has been the main conclusion of the manifold activities carried out by the International Foundation for Development Alternatives between 1978 and 1991.[9]

In more recent years, I have been involved with the negotiated and contractual management of natural resources in the rain tropics coupled with the search for a modern biomass-based civilization[10] and a renewed effort at reconceptualizing development as *the actualization* of all human rights.

[6] For my personal debt to M. Kalecki, see Sachs, I. (1977 and 1999).

[7] Chakravarty, S. (1993).

[8] 'What Now?' (1975).

[9] See in particular, Nerfin, M. (1987). The 81 IFDA Dossiers constitute a unique source of information on alternative development thinking throughout the world.

[10] In association with the South–South Cooperation Programme on Environmentally Sound Socio-Economic Development in the Humid Tropics,

All these preoccupations are underlying the papers assembled in this volume.

This is my fourth book published in India, a matter of great satisfaction to me, as my whole thinking on development was to a great extent shaped by what I observed and learned in this country, where I spent three eventful years from 1957 to 1960.[11] India's unique experience in her search for the *middle path* and democratic planning[12] played an important role in our work on mixed underdeveloped economies, carried out in Warsaw under the guidance of M. Kalecki from 1960 to 1968. At the School of Advanced Social Studies in Paris which I joined in 1968 I had the benefit of interacting with Daniel and Alice Thorner.

I am a firm believer in the virtue of comparative method. In a sense, the social scientist always compares different points in space or in time, or else uses as the term of comparison a paradigm, a type or a norm. Comparison should not necessarily aim at higher level generalizations. Its usefulness mainly comes from what I call the *mirror effect*: by looking at the other, one understands better his own case. Brazil and India have been my two mirrors in the study of development.[13]

Since my youth I have been fascinated by Gandhi and, later on, by the blending in India of the Nehruvian and Gandhian heritages, the scientific temper and the social sensitivity, allied to the commitment to an economy of permanence, and the ethical belief in the ultimate human capacity for self-restraint and a reasonable appreciation of how much is enough.

My gratitude goes to the Indian teachers, colleagues and friends who have guided me in my discovery of India, in particular B. N. Ganguli, V. B. Singh, K. N. Raj, A. K. Sen, Yoginder Alagh,

---

promoted by the Man and the Biosphere Programme of UNESCO, together with the United Nations University and the Third World Academy of Sciences.

[11] For an account of these years, see Sachs, I. (1995).

[12] There is still much to learn from this experience summarized by Chakravarty, S. (1987). See on this point Sachs, I. (1994b).

[13] It is a matter of regret to me that till date, I have not succeeded in organizing a comparison in depth of the Indian and Brazilian trajectories in the second half of the twentieth century with the collaboration of Indian and Brazilian researchers. For a modest beginning, see Sachs, I. (1988).

Deepak Nayyar among the economists, A. Parthasarathi, A. Khosla, M. S. Swaminathan, R. Guha, M. Gadgil, S. Singh among the environmentalists, and Rajni Kothari, my companion-in-dreams about another development, at the International Foundation for Development Alternatives and the United Nations University.

References

Asian Development Bank Review (1998), vol. 30, nr. 4.

Chakravarty, S. (1987), *Development Planning: The Indian Experience*, Clarendon Press, Oxford.

———— (1993), 'M. Kalecki and Development Economics', *Selected Economic Writings*, Oxford University Press, Delhi, Oxford, New York, pp. 234–46.

Nerfin, M. (1987), 'Neither Prince nor Merchant: Citizen—An Introduction to the Third System', *Development Dialogue*, nr. 1, pp. 170–95.

Sachs, I. (1963), *Patterns of Public Sector in Underdeveloped Economies*, Asia Publishing House, New Delhi.

———— (1966), *Foreign Trade and Economic Development of Underdeveloped Countries*, Asia Publishing House, New Delhi.

———— (1977), 'Kalecki and Development Planning' (Michal Kalecki Memorial Lectures), *Oxford Bulletin of Economics and Statistics*, February.

———— (1979), *Studies in Political Economy of Development*, Pergamon Press, Oxford.

———— (1987), *Development and Planning*, Cambridge University Press/ Editions de la Maison des Sciences de l'Homme, Cambridge.

———— (1988), *Historie, culture et styles de développement: Brésil et Inde: esquisse de comparaison*, Sous la dir. de C. Coméliau et I. Sachs, Paris, l'Harmattan; UNESCO/CETRAL.

———— (1993), *Transition Strategies towards the 21st Century* (with a foreword by Maurice F. Strong), Interest Publications for Research and Information System for the Non-Aligned and Other Developing Countries, New Delhi.

———— (1994a) (in collaboration with V. Gowariker), 'Redefining the Good Society: A North–South Dialogue on Challenges of 21st Century', *Economic and Political Weekly*, 4 June, pp. 1383–5.

———— (1994b), L'Inde et l'actualité des voies médianes, *Economie Appliquée* tome XI, VII, n° 2, Grenoble, pp. 181–9.

———— (1995), 'My Education in Delhi', in Kumar, Dharma and Mookherjee, Dilip (eds), *D. School: Reflections on the Delhi School of Economics*, Oxford University Press, Delhi, pp. 68–73.

———— (1999), 'Learning Political Economy with Michal Kalecki', *Review of Political Economy,* July (forthcoming).

Stiglitz, J. E. (1998a), 'More Investments and Broader Goals: Moving towards the Post-Washington Consensus', *WIDER Annual Lecture,* January, Helsinki.

———— (1998b), 'Towards a New Paradigm for Development: Strategies, Policies and Processes', *Prebisch Lecture, 1998* at UNCTAD, Geneva, 19 October.

'What Now?' (1975), Dag Hammarskjöld Report on Development and International Cooperation, *Development Dialogue,* nr. 1/2.

World Bank (1998), *Global Economic Prospects and the Developing Countries 1998/99, Beyond Financial Crisis,* Washington, D. C.

1

Searching for New
Development Strategies
The Challenges of the Social Summit

The United Nations convened a World Summit for Social Development, at Copenhagen, in March 1995. The date is highly symbolic because 1995 marked the 50th anniversary of the dropping of the atom bomb on Hiroshima, the end of the Second World War and the establishment of the United Nations. The Summit provided an opportunity to draw up a balance sheet, both positive and negative, of the past half-century and ask how it may be possible to influence the course of events over the next 50 years and achieve results that progress towards the two essential goals of the United Nations: peace and development.

The Past Half-century

The minuses in the balance sheet outweigh the pluses since the period following the Second World War has been marked throughout by a succession of bloody conflicts waged on political, ethnic, even religious bases and by institutionalized violence, numerous violations of fundamental rights, the imposition of authoritarian regimes and sham democratic practices.

During the Cold War, the balance of terror between the two superpowers averted catastrophies such as a world conflict and consequent nuclear holocaust. The end of the Cold War has not permanently removed this danger but considerably reduced its probability. At the same time, there has been a significant increase in the number of local conflicts. Our century is coming to a close with a new wave of genocidal acts in Africa, and in the very heart of Europe, which is experiencing a revival of the horrors of the two world wars, the extermination camps and the Gulags. At the same time, there have been two major upheavals at the geopolitical level: firstly, the decolonization and emancipation of colonized and dependent countries,[1] and secondly the collapse of real socialism in 1989 followed by the break up of the Soviet Union. To this must be added the end of the apartheid regime in South Africa in 1994 and the still uncertain hopes of lasting peace in the Middle East.

Decolonization and the collapse of real socialism are two irreversible historic turning points with consequences and sequels that continue to weigh heavily on our present. Beyond exaggerated simplifications that seek to replace the bipolar pattern of the Cold War by a so-called shock of civilizations, it must be said that the search for identity is a fertile breeding ground for the rise of dangerously anachronistic forms of ethno-nationalism and fundamentalism. The Polish historian Witold Kula (1960) defined underdevelopment as a *coexistence of asynchronisms*. From this viewpoint, we may speak of a fairly widespread process of involution or *dedevelopment* that is simultaneous with the manifestations of globalization whose economic and social impact, in its differentiated forms, both positive and negative, calls for in-depth assessment. To cast a uniformly positive light on globalization processes would smack of a theology of the market and cannot be part of any scientific analysis.

The period that we have just lived through has seen an unprecedented expansion of technological power, production of goods and services as well as trade. Consumption patterns and lifestyles have been profoundly transformed for a majority of the inhabitants of the industrialized countries and a minority of those of the Third World countries, but the economic improvements indicated by growing statistical averages have not been broadly distributed. In

[1] The main dates to be noted are:

1947: Indian independence,

1949: the victory of the Chinese Revolution,

1955: the Conference of Solidarity of Asian and African countries in Bandung,

1960: African decolonization.

10   *Understanding Development*

as rich a country as France, a *societal fracture* is now creating a divide
between the two-thirds constituting the winners and the third who
are the losers and are increasingly excluded from the consumer
society and deprived of their (nonetheless fundamental) right to
work. In other words, France too has its 'Fourth World' and the
South is present in the North. The privileged minority in the Third
World countries, on the other hand, forms a presence of the North
in the South without there being any territorially demarcated
enclaves. The North and the South are in contact and are interpen-
etrating each other, especially in the big cities.

The world has shrunk because of the improvements in trans-
port and, to an even more significant extent, because of the
communications revolution.[2] These technical advances are the
basis of the already mentioned manifestations of globalization that
are occurring at an uneven pace in fields as varied as those of
finance, economics, technology and culture.

We are living through a period of the *decoupling of the financial
economy from the real economy* (Drucker, 1986), the consequence
of which is the establishment of circuits of financial speculation
that drain away capital which could otherwise have financed
productive investment and helped create jobs. Transnational firms
have become the main agents in the economy and in trade to such
a significant extent that production and international trade statistics in the form of national aggregates have been made obsolete.

The media everywhere are propagating an identical picture of
the good life based on unbridled consumption and the Hollywood
dream. A small minority of men and women travel with ease all
over the planet, to the extent that tourism and travel have become
a major sector of the economy.[3] However, the majority of the
inhabitants of our planet continue to live as if they were *glebae*

[2] The almost exclusive attention paid to advances in the audio-visual sector
has diverted attention from the second Gutenberg revolution which is taking
place under our very eyes and is opening up extraordinary possibilities for the
production of school books and textbooks. We refer to the very substantial
drop in the cost of production of books printed on a large scale. Italian editions
of 100 page books selling for 1000 lire have been followed by English and then
French editions of major classics of several hundreds of pages, selling for £ 1
and 10 francs.

[3] According to Naisbitt (1995, pp. 132–3) tourism and travel provide
employment to 204 million people throughout the world and correspond to

adscripti. There is a striking contrast between the restrictions on the international mobility of labour and the increasing mobility of other factors of production.

Distribution of economic activity, 1991 (percentage of world total)

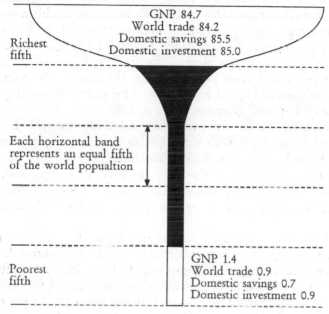

GNP 84.7
World trade 84.2
Domestic savings 85.5
Domestic investment 85.0

Richest fifth

Each horizontal band represents an equal fifth of the world popualtion

Poorest fifth

GNP 1.4
World trade 0.9
Domestic savings 0.7
Domestic investment 0.9

Fig. 1.1 The cup of shame
Source: UNDP, *World Report on Human Development, 1994*.

Science and technology are very imperfectly controlled. Prometheus got entangled, to borrow a metaphor from Jean-Jacques Salomon (1984).[4] The destructive power of technologies, the uses of which continue to be subordinated to the search for short-term financial and economic profit, has furthermore brought about the

---

10.2 per cent of the world's GNP. Nearly 11 per cent of expenditure by consumers is allocated to tourism and travel. Naisbitt very optimistically puts the number of new jobs that will be created in these sectors up to the year 2005 at 144 million. Nearly half of these jobs correspond to the Asia-Pacific region.
[4] See also Salomon, J. J. (1992), Salomon, J. J., F. Sagasti and C. Sachs-Jeantet (eds) (1994) and the essay by Ruffolo, Giorgio (1988).

deterioration of the environment. The wise management of this has become an imperative for the world, as was seen at the Earth Summit in Rio de Janeiro in 1992.

Above all, scientific and technical progress has not kept its promise of widespread well-being for the whole of mankind. In 1930, Keynes expected that mankind's economic problem would be definitively resolved within a century. Man, for the first time since his emergence on our planet, would then be able to face his real, his permanent problem: 'how to use his freedom from pressing economic cares, how to occupy the leisure, which science and...compound interest will have won for him, to live wisely and agreeably and well' (Keynes, 1972, p. 328).

We henceforth have the technological ability to provide each and every individual with a reasonable degree of material comfort. According to two World Bank data, the world's average per capita income was nearly $ 4300 in 1992. By comparison, the per capita income in the United Kingdom was $ 4593 in 1900 and that of the United States at the same period was $ 4096 (Maddison, 1994).

However, the inequality that characterizes the distribution of incomes among different countries and within each country divests this statistical average of any meaning. In 1991, the richest fifth of the world's population appropriated 84.7 per cent of the world's GNP while the share of the poorest fifth was limited to 1.4 per cent. Within a span of 30 years, the disparity between the incomes of these two extreme groups went up from 30/1 to 60/1.

Even more significant is the fact, that in modern societies, *exclusion is gaining ground over exploitation*. The rich no longer need the poor. This is probably why they tend to forget them.[5]

---

[5] This is what has been denounced by Rajni Kothari. See Kothari, Rajni (1993). For his part, Jacques Delors has said: 'We are already living, alas, in a society that gets upset about injustice and from time to time takes part in televised charity shows, gives money and then for the rest of the time is complacent. This is ghastly but it is what we are increasingly threatened with'. Interview with *Le Monde*, 15 November 1994. See also Wolfe Marshall (1994, p. 1) for whom the word 'exclusion' indicates the superfluity of the excluded as opposed to their incorporation into the economy under conditions of exploitation. In a very recent and seminal work on the disintegration of the wage-earning society and to the metamorphoses of the social question, Robert Castel (1995, p. 22) prefers the term *social disablement*.

The increasingly unequal distribution of the products of technical and economic progress arises out of faulty social and political organization and not out of any scarcity of goods. It throws up a challenge to the political establishment which is incapable of making efficient use of technological power (Ruffolo, 1988). We are here at the very heart of the notion of *maldevelopment* (Sachs, 1984) which is not incompatible with economic growth, even at high rates. The fact of the matter is that growth and development are not synonymous. So long as huge social disparities persist, growth will certainly be a necessary but *in no way sufficient* condition of development, for the distributive and qualitative aspects cannot be overlooked. It is not true to say that the exorbitantly high social and ecological costs of certain forms of economic growth are the unavoidable 'ravages of progress'.

Whom does such progress benefit? This question permeates the three points of the Copenhagen Summit agenda: the struggle against poverty, social integration and the creation of productive jobs. It is neither acceptable nor necessary that financial and economic progress should be paid for by structural unemployment and underemployment which lead to increasingly widespread manifestations of social exclusion and poverty. The way in which the agenda for Copenhagen has been structured, and this was also the case with the Earth Summit in 1992, is an implicit rejection of the narrow economic theories that make growth the central if not the only goal. It also tolls the knell of the belief that the benefits of economic growth will almost automatically spread to the whole society. In the words of Louis Emmerij (1994):

...no one can question the fact that economic growth is, in the long term, effective in achieving social goals and combating poverty, but three to five generations may be necessary to reach this goal. In other words, the transition period will be humanly unbearable and politically irresponsible.

This is why it is necessary to deal with the five themes of peace, economy, environment, justice and democracy all at the same time, in taking social conditions as the starting point for efforts towards development.[6] The present text is far more limited in its aim. It

[6] On this subject, see the report by the UN Secretary-General. 'Development and International Economic Co-operation—An Agenda for Development', document A/48/935 dated 6 May 1994 as well as the Position Paper

seeks only to analyse those aspects of the problem of development that appear to merit special attention. In the following pages, after examining the worldwide social crisis with special emphasis on integration into the production process through employment and self-employment, we shall look at the search for new paradigms of development through the following issues: going beyond 'economicism', the need for a universal postulate, the relations between the economic, the ecological and the social, the democratic regulation of mixed economies, the redefinition of the role of the State, new forms of partnership among the different social actors, science and technology in the service of social development and reforms in the international system.

The Widespread Social Crisis

A widespread social crisis, in different forms and with different degrees of intensity, is affecting (with few exceptions) the Third World countries, East European countries and the former Soviet Union (today known as countries in transition), and even the industrial countries.

In the Third World, the poor, who are the victims of the underdevelopment of productive capacities, have been joined by the new poor, who are the victims of a mimetic concept of modernity based on the transposition of the latest techniques coming from the industrialized countries. It is true that there is need for a selective use of such techniques. However, the indiscriminate opening up of the economies of the South creates the risk of intensifying the process of the dualization of the economy and society with a resulting increase in the numbers of those excluded and a threat, in the long run, of social apartheid. The countries in transition have to cope simultaneously with a threefold challenge. They have to stabilize their economies, create from scratch all the institutions necessary for the functioning of market-led economies and, finally, carry out a thorough restructuring of their productive capacities in order to increase their efficiency, competitiveness in international markets and performance in the management of the environment. In many respects, therefore, the problems of the

---

by the Director-General of UNESCO: 'Towards the Preparation of the World Summit for Social Development', UNESCO, 29 July 1994.

countries in transition resemble those of the countries of the Third World.[7]

A transformation of this nature cannot be achieved without high social costs. However, the choice of a strategy based on the illusion that it is possible to achieve the instant establishment of capitalism and the sovereign rule of the market economy seems to have increased these costs and, furthermore, to have prolonged their existence beyond what is necessary. The worsening of social relations, the deterioration of health, education and welfare services, the emergences of massive structural unemployment which will be difficult to absorb, the vulnerability of the countries in transition to the shock of a far too sudden opening up of their economies, the permissivity in regard to the practices of savage capitalism, are all so many factors that weigh down on the negative side of the balance sheet of the great transformation, at least for the time being.

However, the most astonishing aspect of the current social crisis is the deterioration of the condition of the industrial countries, after decades of fast economic and technical progress.

It might almost be said that we are seeing these countries slide into a Third World status. Indeed, the intellectual tools that were earlier fashioned to study the economic and social dualization of the post-colonial countries and account for the phenomena of social exclusion and spatial segregation have returned in a big way to the heated debate, now going on in most of the industrialized countries. Unemployment, the precariousness of jobs and the various forms of exclusion resulting therefrom have become endemic. No one is hoodwinked by the euphemism of 'two-speed society'. Marshall Wolfe (1994) distinguishes several forms of exclusion, relating to the means of livelihood; social services, protection services and security networks; consumer culture; the process of making political choices: the bases of popular and solidarity organizations; and finally the capacity to understand what is happening.

Events therefore are all running counter to what the optimistic theories of development led us to believe. What we are witnessing

---

[7] In its analysis of the global economy published in its edition dated 1 October 1994, *The Economist* lumped together the economies of the Third World, the Eastern European countries and the former Soviet Union under the term 'developing countries' as opposed to the 'rich industrial countries'.

is not the disappearance of the traditional sector by the gradual transfer of its redundant labour force to the modern sector but the expulsion of surplus workers from the modern sector into the 'informal', 'grey' or quite simply 'black' sectors of the economy, or even their pure and simple reduction to marginal status, condemning them to the pangs of enforced idleness and to the status of dole recipients—in some cases from the cradle to the grave.

At a time when we have greatest need of it, the Welfare State is under attack and is even being partially dismantled on the pretext of its excessive cost and bureaucratic unwieldiness and the supposed efficiency of alternative formulas, postulating the commodification of social services. It is true that the methods by which Welfare States function must change. However, it must not be forgotten that they are the only truly positive contribution that Europe has made to the world in the twentieth century, being the result of a century and a half of social struggle, and also of competition with real socialism at a time when the latter still enjoyed credibility in the eyes of a significant part of Western public opinion.

More than ever, the goals of full employment and of comprehensive and adequate social protection represent a basic part of the European identity. Instead of defending welfare entitlements and other social rights in their present form, it is necessary to place on the agenda a thorough reform of the Welfare States without, in any way, relieving them of responsibilities by relying solely on market mechanisms. The direction that this reform should take is clear. People have to be helped to take responsibility for themselves, with the assistance of the State. This must be done through a search for many varied forms of partnership for the production of social services between users, the civil society represented by associations and the other components of the social economy (co-operatives and mutual benefit societies), administrative bodies at all levels from the local to the national and, finally, private enterprises.[8]

The three points on the agenda of the Copenhagen Conference were closely interlinked. It would seem however that, logically,

[8] Cf. Balbo, Laura (1994). 'From Welfare State to Caring Society', contribution prepared for the International Conference on Public Policies, Peoples' Actions and Social Development organized by UNESCO, the University and City of Bologna, Bologna, 2–3 December 1994.

priority should have been given to the implementation of pro-active policies that strike at the very root of the problem by integration into the productive process through employment or self-employment. Policies of assistance in which the poor are cared for are certainly necessary, given the size and urgency of the problem of poverty. However, such policies by themselves will not bring lasting solutions. The excluded receiving assistance will continue to be excluded so long as they do not find a place in the economy.

Similarly, social integration which brings numerous cultural factors and forms of social organization into play depends to a major degree on the capacity to provide all the different compo-nents of the population, beyond their social, ethnic or religious differences and their level of education, with the conditions that will enable them to earn a decent livelihood by their work.

The *population explosion* is often presented as the main cause of the acute underemployment and unemployment prevailing in the countries of the South. However, this thesis needs to be qualified by a closer look at the population–development loop. As long as the populations of the South have not acquired security in terms of food and social protection, have high infant mortality rates and continue to receive inadequate education, especially in the case of girls, it will be difficult to convince them that birth control policies are well-founded. Their partial rationality, limited to the family unit, will continue to run counter to global rationality. The demo-graphic transition cannot be achieved without social development based on integration into the productive process.

The priority that must be attached to the problem of employ-ment and self employment is all the greater as enforced idleness[9] is an irreversible form of destruction of human life, for time lost

---

[9] Enforced idleness is quite the opposite of the revolution of liberated time released through advances in productivity inasmuch as this revolution implies a reduction in the heteronomous working time of people who have already been socialized by work. Ivan Illich (1977) and André Gorz (1988) have very well shown how this released time could be used for autonomous economic and non-economic activities and thus contribute to cultural enrichment and the fullness of life. However, the deliberately provocative title of Illich's book, *Creative Unemployment*, lends itself to confusion. For a discussion of the revolution of liberated time, see also Echanges et Projets (1980), Sachs (1984) and Aznar (1993).

can be neither stored nor retrieved. The real challenge is to break the dynamic chain of unemployment and exclusion and replace it with the dynamics of employment (Brunhes, 1993). The scale of the problem can be seen from a reading of the available statistics and projections.

The International Labour Organization has prepared projections of the economically active population (EAP) for the period 1985–2025, which we shall use to assess the magnitude of the number of jobs that have to be created and are necessary to absorb newcomers to the job markets in the present decade and the next two decades without taking account of the need to absorb existing unemployment (ILO, 1986).

TABLE 1.1
Increase in EAP (ILO projections in millions)

	1990	2000	2010	2020
Less developed regions	360	383	352	
More developed regions	29	11	−0.4	
World	389	394	351.5	

Indeed, as Table 1.1 shows, from 1990 to the year 2000, the active population should increase by 389 million and then, in the first two decades of the twenty-first century, by 394 million and 351.5 million respectively. Most of the new jobs to be created are likely to be in the less developed regions: 92.5 per cent of the total increase between 1990 and 2000, 97 per cent between 2000 and 2010, more than 100 per cent between 2010 and 2020, since during this latter period the EAP of the most developed regions will shrink by 400 thousand.

The data do not take already existing unemployment and underemployment into account. About 30 per cent of the world's active population is in this condition according to United Nations estimates. The absorption of this section would require the creation of very many additional jobs. According to the International Commission for Peace and Food, to ensure full employment, it would be necessary to create about a billion new jobs during the present decade (1994, p. 71).

According to the ILO data, the condition of the most developed regions appears to be comfortable at first sight, since the annual growth rate of their EAP will be barely 0.49 per cent during the present decade and 0.34 per cent during the next decade. Creating some 3 million jobs a year should not raise any problems given that, according to World Bank data, gross investment in high income countries in 1991 amounted to $ 3750 billion (as compared with $ 1010 billion for the rest of the world).

However, this does not at all represent the true picture. Instead of creating jobs, investment in productive capacities is tending rather to replace men by machines. In many branches of industry, the relationship between growth and employment is becoming a negative one. The race for competitivity is resulting in rates of growth in productivity that are higher than rates of growth in production. To take only one especially telling example, between 1980 and 1992, Spain doubled its Gross Domestic Product without creating a single additional job. We are therefore in a structurally novel situation that is the result of a combination of several factors. We shall mention four of them.

The facts have belied the optimistic expectations of those who, in preaching the virtues of the permanent race for technological innovation (Riboud, 1987), promised a growth in employment in the modern services sector that would exceed the loss of direct jobs in factories through automation. Recent advances in office automation point to the same trend towards replacing men by machines in the tertiary sector.

The link between production and employment is loosening and intensive growth is taking precedence over extensive growth. As far as France is concerned, E. Malinvaud expects a growth rate of 3 per cent in the long term accompanied by an annual 1 per cent increase in employment and an annual 0.5 per cent drop in unemployment.[10]

This major trend in the present phase of technological development goes hand in hand with a decoupling of the real economy from the financial economy, whose explosive expansion marks the end of the twentieth century (Drucker, 1986). As already pointed out, the capital that could have been invested productively is being diverted by the lure of spectacular gain to the gambling tables of the 'global casino' that the financial markets have become. The sterilization of this capital is slowing down the growth of the real economy.

[10] Interview with *Le Monde*, 16 November 1993.

The industrial societies, dominated by the ideology of consumerism, have been unable to take advantage of the growth in productivity to carry out the drastic reduction of working time, which is a social necessity. It is true that whereas work took up 200,000 hours in the lifetime of a Frenchman at the end of the nineteenth century, it now takes up only 70,000 hours (Rigaudiat, 1993). However, the objective conditions for accelerating this trend now exist. From Kropotkin to Gorz and Illich, not to mention Bertrand Russell and Keynes, many thinkers have made proposals for a revolution of liberated time and a reorganization of society enabling people to work less in order to procure work for all, to paraphrase the title of a recent book (Aznar, 1993).

The present crisis seems to favour a resumption of this debate whose ethical and cultural dimensions go beyond the technical modalities of an initial reduction of working time. The implementation of a policy of equitable redistribution of the socially needed work calls for a genuine cultural revolution and for profound institutional changes.[11] The situation can, however, be improved through a modification of the fiscal and parafiscal policies that increase the cost of labour through social security contributions. These contributions could be financed in other ways, for example by a tax on equipment or by an appropriately modulated Value Added Tax.

The recent trends in economic thinking dominated by neoliberal theories explain the inadequacy of employment policies and, more generally, of public policies concerning development.

The decline and then the collapse of real socialism have been interpreted as the green light for returning to an unbridled form of capitalism whose success is measured by rising stock exchange indexes and volumes of profits, and no longer by the creation of jobs. Stringent rules on adjustment of macroeconomic and monetary balances and on liberalization have been laid down by the International Monetary Fund and the World Bank, protecting the creditors of the debtor countries. Notwithstanding disclaimers by the IMF and the World Bank, the austerity policies dictate heavy

---

[11] Nor are there any grounds for expecting a major creation of jobs through the replacement of wage-earning work by forms of workers' participation in profits (the notion of the sharing economy) as postulated by J. Meade (1986) or M. L. Weitzmann (1985). In this respect, see Brunetta, R. (1994).

sacrifices on the part of the most underprivileged social classes.[12] Deregulation, privatization and budgetary austerity have been used, with the pretext of curbing the excesses of statism, to restrict the field of action of States and buttress the position of large private companies, both national and foreign. The same strategy, barring a few details, has been proposed for the countries in transition towards the market economy.

The failure of the industrialized countries to reduce unemployment despite the financial resources at their disposal provides a measure of the scale of the challenge facing the less developed countries. During the present decade, they will have to create twelve times as many jobs merely to absorb newcomers to the job market with a gross fixed capital formation that is four times smaller! One immediate conclusion needs to be drawn. It is quite unthinkable that the models of the North can be reproduced in the countries of the South. No longer can these countries, in the name of competitivity and of integration into the global economy, accept the infernal pace of 'creative destruction' that even the richest countries are unable to keep up with.

And yet this is the path chosen by the elites of the Third World. We can understand the vehemence with which Kothari (1993) has criticized them in his already quoted book, where he proposes that India should take an approach to development based on social empowerment, decentralized planning and job promotion, rather than on growth as such, an approach based on the development of the countryside and the expansion of the internal market rather than on giving excessive priority to exports. Of his proposals, we would single out the emphasis laid on the need to consider employment as a key variable in development strategies. A finely tuned employment policy, prepared on the basis of field data, would therefore appear to be an essential part of the public policies to which we shall return later.[13] While recognizing the seriousness of the situation, we feel that there is room for manoeuvre in this field, provided that a thorough review is made of the goals and methods of development. When Alice in

[12] As Anizur Rahman Khan has prudently stated (1993, p. 67): 'it is very difficult to offer convincing proof that the programmes of adjustment have succeeded in protecting the interest of the poor'.

[13] For more details, see Sachs, I. (1994).

Wonderland politely asked the Cheshire-cat to kindly tell her where she was to go from the place she was in, the cat replied: 'That depends a great deal on where you want to get to.'

Development Reconsidered

The already cited report by the International Commission for Peace and Food (1994), rightly considers the search for new development paradigms to be among the major priorities of the present time. East European statism has collapsed but there is no place for unfettered capitalism either. 'Rather than searching for a victor and vanquished, the urgent need is to find a successor that combines and synthesises the enlightened values of both systems' (p. 154). The well-being of all individuals should determine social policy and the market economies should undertake to guarantee the right of every citizen to employment.

The report adopts the UN Secretary-General's view that the most important intellectual challenge in the coming years will be that of the renewal of development thinking. The world has sufficient experience and information to formulate an integrated theory of development seen as a social process centred on man as a whole and on all men. The Social Summit should set the ball rolling.

The task is a difficult one. It requires firstly recognizing the fact that there is a widespread social crisis which, as we have already seen, affects in different ways and with different degrees of intensity, every group of countries, including the industrialized ones.

Going beyond 'Economicism'

Furthermore, this task makes it necessary to go beyond 'economicism' which is still the dominant thinking and is expressed by the explicit or implicit acceptance of the trickle-down theory. According to this theory, it is the economy that rules. What needs to be done essentially therefore is to ensure the macroeconomic controls that enable reasonable growth, and the rest will follow of its own accord. The benefits resulting from this growth will ultimately flow into the entire fabric of society and spread to the very base of the pyramid. The agenda of the Earth Summit and, even more so, that of the Social Summit implicitly deny the trickle-down theory, but the practice of many governments continues to be based on this theory and the most extreme neoliberal currents of thought preach it openly.

Another element of mainstream thinking overestimates the importance of competitiveness, which has been raised to the status of a real ideology, based on a *superficial theory of globalization*, presented purely in its positive aspects, as if increases in financial, commercial and technical flows always occur in such a way as to benefit each and every partner including the weakest. The concept of interdependence is often pushed to the fore in order to avoid any analysis of the degree of asymmetry, even domination, that exists in the relationships between strong partners and weak partners. The Report of the Group of Lisbon (1993) has come out strongly against the ideology of competitiveness and has demonstrated its limits.[14]

As for globalization, we may note first of all that it is occurring unequally in different fields. As historians have shown, the microbial unification of the world took place before the birth of the world market!

We have already pointed out that the financial markets, working round the clock and seven days of the week, put in motion monetary flows quite out of proportion to the needs of the real economy. The lure of easy, albeit risky, gains ultimately sterilizes a substantive part of the resources that could have taken the form of productive investment. It is currently estimated that the transactions made on the foreign exchange markets amount to a thousand billion dollars a day. James Tobin's ingenious proposal, made as early as 1978, for taxing currency transfers at a rate of 0.5 per cent, would bring in more than $ 1500 billion per year which could be used for development purposes. Despite the obvious advantages of this proposal and its adoption by the influential United Nations Development Programme *World Report on Human Development* (1994, p. 75), there is no great likelihood of it being seriously looked at in Copenhagen, or elsewhere.

Globalization is taking great strides in the field of communications. Identical television programmes are reaching all corners of

[14] See also Petrella, Ricardo (1994). Contrary to R. Reich (1992), Paul Krugmann (1994) is, among American economists, the one who has most clearly seen the danger of giving excessive importance to competition for external markets to the detriment of the fundamental question of the development of the domestic market.

the globe with a tendency towards a homogenization of culture that is raising problems (Ortiz, 1994) and, even more seriously, paving the way for a *telecracy*, a term invented by the French daily, *Le Monde*, in the aftermath of Silvio Berlusconi's election victory in Italy.

The post-War period was marked by an expansion of trade and technological exchanges that was greater than the economic growth rates, and therefore also by an opening up of economies. Once again, the picture needs to be qualified, since the degree of opening differed greatly from one country to another. In particular, continent-sized countries compensate for relatively low levels of foreign trade by internal trade. The place of the United States in world trade is a result, not of a high degree of opening up, but of the size of its GDP.

Certain ideologists of globalization like John Naisbitt (1995) strive to show that the advance of globalization gives an increasingly significant advantage to networks of small partners which enjoy a degree of flexibility that States and large firms do not possess. There is some truth in Naisbitt's approach when he speaks of the retreat, in terms of identity, of the Nation-State towards what he calls 'the tribes'. According to him, one of the aspects of the global paradox is precisely the fact that the more universal we become, the more tribal we act (p. 24). In the course of his explanation, the author underestimates the increasingly dominant role, in the world economy, of transnational corporations which are constantly increasing their power while the influence of States gets blurred and while international institutions have practically no way of controlling the practices of these companies.

The ultimate thrust of his book lies, however, in its unexpected extolling of the advent of the age of individualism marking the end of politics as we know it, and hence in its minimizing or even its elimination of the State's responsibility with respect to its social functions, notably as regards employment. 'Now with the electronics revolution, both representative democracy and economies of scale are obsolete. Now everyone can have efficient direct democracy' (p. 47). The communications networks are supposed to take care of this.

Yet, as Oliver Dollfus (1994) has stressed, the system that produces the World-Space creates forms of participation in as well as exclusion from the process of globalization.[15]. Furthermore, globalization is based on a vision that underestimates the variety of historical experiences and the plurality of humankind. This is why in most places it is arousing its contrary, namely the development of particularism. In reality, as Bertrand Badie (1994; see also Badie and Smouts, 1992) has persuasively shown, we are moving towards a New World Disorder because of a threefold break marked by globalization, the crisis of the Nation-State and the end of bipolarity. Today's forms of opposition are no longer ideological but cultural. The present-day world is characterized by the failure of three fetish concepts of modern international relations: sovereignty, territoriality and security. Insofar as nationalism is being weakened in favour of micro-communalism and macro-social forms of solidarity (*inter alia* of a religious type), the 'international' order enters a stage of crisis.

Another characteristic of dominant economic thinking is that it considers itself to be universally valid. This actually gives it an *ahistoric* and *atopic* character. In practice, it amounts to denying a field proper to the theories of development and to maintaining, in the face of all evidence to the contrary, that the mimetic transposition of the experiences of the industrial countries to the rest of the world constitutes the right path to development. The prohibitive social costs of the structural adjustment policies applied uniformly throughout the planet are once again denying this claim, without there being any change in the practices of the international organizations based on the 'Washington Consensus'.[16]

The idea of the plurality of developmental paths is increasingly on the development agenda. The development strategies must take into account certain *specific characteristics common to several*

---

[15] Dollfus has written: 'A new form of exclusion arises with the world economy and market: the exclusion of the "useless", of those who cannot or do not wish to sell their abilities and their labour force, who, because of their poverty, do not have purchasing power that is sufficiently worthwhile for the market. "Useless" individuals are localized in entire regions of the world as well as right within societies that are considered to be prosperous' (p. 9).

[16] For an analysis of the most striking characteristics of policies based on the principles of the Washington Consensus in the Indian context, see: Nayyar, Deepak (1993) and Taylor, Lance (1994). See also Comeliau, Christian (1994).

countries (for example large countries and countries rich in natural resources as opposed to small countries and countries poor in natural resources), thus making it possible to establish certain heuristic typologies.[17] On the other hand, they must account for the *singular features of each country:*

- the historical and cultural context, it being necessary to understand development as a dynamic process.[18]

- the ecological context, since climatic and biological diversity, when well interpreted, yield a potential of resources that can be used for development without destroying the capital of nature, the link between natural diversity and cultural diversity being very close. After all, an important aspect of culture is the knowledge that a society has of its natural environment.[19]

- finally the institutional context, in the broad sense of the term, reflecting the organization of human society.

In the face of the multiple paths of the past, present and future, what can be expected of a theory of development is a comparative analysis of accumulated experiences, both positive and negative, capable of stimulating the social imagination without delivering ready-made models for all that.

We feel that a normative discourse is indispensable in order to evolve a mobilizing *national project*, based on an explicit set of values recognizing the living burden of the past but oriented towards the future. A project of this kind will additionally have a very important function of serving as a criterion for the assessment of policies proposed and of paths taken. The notions of rationality and efficiency lose their precision when there is no strategic planning oriented towards the medium and the long term. Without repeating, yet again, the errors of comprehensive

[17] These typologies should serve as a referential system for an examinaton of concrete historical cases and must not be taken as a set of boxes in which different countries may be separately classified.

[18] The historian and the developer have much in common, except that the historian interprets the past which has already taken place while the developer seeks to influence the course of the future. The interdisciplinary and comparative approaches of the kind practised by historians contain precious lessons for the developers.

[19] 'Resourcefulness' is a key concept in eco-development.

planning made by the centralized economies it is necessary, on the contrary, drawing upon all the lessons of past failures, to undertake flexible, dialogue-based,[20] contextual and contractual planning.

The Search for Universal Values

In a world where, as we have seen, particular cultural identities are assuming increasing importance, the question is whether it is possible to set up a universal postulate.

Our answer would be affirmative, in the light of the debate inaugurated by the Stockholm Conference in 1972 and resumed by the Rio Earth Summit in 1992. We feel that development, in the full sense of the word, should have a social purpose justified by the ethical postulate of intra-generational solidarity and equity, taking the form of a social contract. While the social disparities between nations and within nations have only increased, everything needs to be done to reduce them. This requires privileged groups to ask the question: 'how much is enough?'[21] The development of man as a whole and of all men can become widespread only through the building of *'a civilization of being in an equitable sharing of having'* to quote L. J. Lebret.[22] By contrast, the extrapolation of the current major trends can only accentuate the drift towards social apartheid.

Furthermore, development requires *ecological prudence* in the name of inter-generational solidarity expressed in terms of a natural contract (Serres, 1990).

Finally, at the instrumental level, the *principle of economic efficiency* is a necessary one. However, it must be measured by the macro-social yardstick and no longer solely in terms of profitability at the firm level.

Furthermore, two other principles may be mentioned: cultural acceptability and territorial balance.[23]

[20] The Polish economist J. Hausner (1995), following Scandinavian writers, speaks of the 'negotiated strategy' among the social agents. The experience of French planning has the same thrust.

[21] Here is a truly Gandhian question that applies, nevertheless, primarily to the industrial societies and is found also in a somewhat different form among certain Catholic thinkers; see in particular the Encyclicals of Jean-Paul II (1994). This question has raised a sharp debate in Sweden (see 'What Now?' 1975).

[22] For a selection of his writings, see Economie et Humanisme (1986).

[23] For more details see Sachs, I. (1993).

Development is thus seen as a pluridimensional concept.[24] This fact is reflected in the abuse of the adjectives that accompany the word 'development': economic, social, political, cultural, sustainable, finally human,[25] to mention but a few. It is not too soon to spare ourselves all these attributes by concentrating on a redefinition of the content of the word 'development', based on the proposed hierarchical structure where the social is in control, the ecological is an accepted constraint and the economic is reduced to its instrumental role.

Beyond semantics, a far more formidable problem as regards practice is that of bringing into harmony goals which, at first sight, may appear to be contradictory and hence lead to painful trade-offs.

Economic Development and the Environment

The debate on development and the environment has concentrated essentially on the characteristic situations of a zero-sum game. There has been no sufficient exploration of *win–win* situations which nevertheless exist and could have increased if a search had been made in this direction. The examples that could be given are those of the various cases of recycling, the so-called regenerative agriculture and especially the energy strategies aimed at reducing the consumption of fossil energy while at the same time saving financial resources.[26] The same reasoning can be applied to other resources. The members of the Factor 10 Club call for a tenfold increase in the average productivity of the resources in the industrial economies, in the next half-century, as a prerequisite for sustainable development on a worldwide scale.[27]

[24] Henri Bartoli's work (1991) on the multidimensional economy starts with a reference to Blaise Pascal's view that not only is it impossible to know the parts without knowing the whole, but also to know the whole without knowing specifically the parts.

[25] It is unfortunate that the UNDP has chosen the word 'human' rather than 'humane'.

[26] In this respect, see notably the pioneering book of Goldemberg et al. (1988) and the work of Dessus, Benjamin (1995).

[27] For more details and notably for recommendations on policies to be followed, see the Carnoulès Declaration reproduced in *Development Alternatives Newsletter*, vol. 4, no. 12, December 1994.

The general situation is summarized in Fig. 1.2. The quadrant D represents 'hell'. The quadrant A and C correspond to zero-sum games. In the quadrant A, the improvement of the state of the environment comprises economic costs that are expressed by a deceleration of growth. The quadrant B is that of the positive-sum game in which the win-win cases occur. At a given time, with the existing technical and organizational knowledge, all the win-win cases may be represented by a curve TT'. The problem is to shift the curve TT' to the right and upwards.

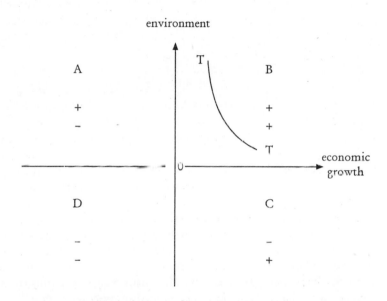

Fig. 1.2 The starting point 0 corresponds to a 'normal' situation of a steady growth rate with a moderately positive economic growth rate and the rate of deterioration of the environment that corresponds to it. What interests us are the variations of these two rates.

Development: Economic and Social

The agenda of the Copenhagen Conference brings into play the relationship between economic and social development while the earlier pattern tacitly assumed that economic growth and social progress went hand in hand. Given the current magnitude

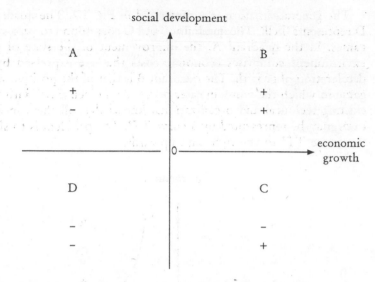

Fig. 1.3 Social and economic growth—the possible situations

of joblessness and the resulting phenomena of exclusion, the relationships between the economic and the social are shown in Fig. 1.3.

The quadrant D, which is unfortunately largely present in the current situation, is the one where the reduction of growth leads to marked social deterioration. The quadrant C corresponds to growth going hand in hand with the reduction in employment and the resultant social degradation. The quadrant A represents the rare situations where economic deterioration does not destroy the micro-social fabric characterized by great cohesion. The quadrant B is, once again, that of the positive-sum game within which there are the win-win cases.

But we must now turn to the *triple-win (or win-win-win)* situations which enable progress on all three fronts together: economic, social and ecological, and therefore bring about development in the full sense of the word.

We propose that the term 'development' should be reserved only for these cases by opposition to the different forms of maldevelopment or of lopsided development. All the relevant situations in terms of economic, social and ecological aspects are summarized in Table 1.2.

TABLE 1.2
Development: The Triple–win Situation

	Economic	Social	Ecological
1. Savage growth	+	–	–
2. Socially benign growth	+	+	–
3. Environmentally sustainable growth	+	–	+
4. Development	+	+	+

The Democratic Regulation of the Mixed Economies

To achieve triple-win solutions, we have to *rethink the institutional framework* in which development is conceived and achieved. Once the two extremes of the pure market economy (a liberal utopia in the etymological sense of the word) and the command economy are set aside, all the real situations that exist in the world belong to the category of *mixed economies*. These are characterized by a wide variety of labour, commodity and service markets operated by private profit-making and public enterprises, as well as by agents of the social economy (co-operatives, mutual benefit societies, associations and non-profit-making private organizations). The population is partly engaged in non-market economic activities carried out in households.[28] For Shigeto Tsuru (1993), the mixed economy is the only mode of production that is still in the race. Jean Saint-Geours (1992) has gone a step further and refers to 'mixity' as a characteristic of our societies beyond the economic field.

Of course, the mixing of the public and private sectors can take many varied forms. Quite significantly, nowadays the search for new forms of articulation, between the different social actors, concerns practically every country of the globe, given the vacuum created by the collapse of real socialism, the crisis in the Welfare States and the more than modest balance-sheet of development/maldevelopment in the South.

The problem is located at the level of what Paul Streeten (1989) calls the *mesoeconomy*, as the neoliberal theories have overestimated, firstly, the role of macro-economic controls (of course

---

[28] The extra-market economy should not be mistaken for the 'informal economy' which is a part of the market economy.

necessary, but in no way sufficient) and, secondly, that of the microeconomic activity of the entrepreneurs. Now, in many places, even today events are all taking place according to a pattern that contradicts the one set forth by Schumpeter: the initiative and the risks are taken by the State, while privatization at a discount subsequently benefits a class of entrepreneurs who have nothing Schumpeterian about them. The three central questions are:

– What State for what development?

– What content should be given to democracy beyond mere compliance with the rules of the game of representative democracy?

– How to achieve new forms of partnership among the State, the civil society and the business world so as to enhance and bring out the full potential of local initiatives and citizen actions?

These questions shall be examined in turn.

What State?

For several reasons, the current debate on the State addresses the wrong questions. Its starting point is the opposition between the State and the market but the fact remains that any market must be regulated by the State, especially if it is desired that the market economy should also fulfil a social function. The criticisms made against statism, which rightly lash out at its excesses and the weight of the bureaucracy, oversimplify the problem by calling for *less* of the State, whereas the real point is that the State should be more efficient and at the same time cost less. It is fashionable to concentrate on State failures and overlook market failures, at times equally numerous, as the market is incapable of grasping the long term and the interests of society. It is legitimate to propose a reduction of the role of the Entrepreneurial State, especially when the public sector consists of firms nationalized at a time when they were bankrupt and when the State, by intervening, furthered the particular interests of some private groups having close links with the establishment. However, there still remain the functions of the developmental State, as in the example of Japan, South Korea and Taiwan,[29] and, last but not the least, the functions of the Regulating State. The challenge in the years to come will be to find truly democratic forms for the regulation of the mixed economies. This brings us to the second question.

Appropriation of All Fundamental Rights

Respect for political rights alone is not sufficient to define a democracy in the full sense of the word. The effective exercising of all political, civic, social, cultural and economic rights should be extended to the entire population, especially to those who are now excluded from enjoying them. These include the right to individual and collective development and, of course, the right to work or to self-employment that provides a decent livelihood earned in dignity. As we have already pointed out, only integration into the productive process is capable, in the immediate future, of striking at the roots of exclusion. Policies of assistance are of course very necessary, given the predicament of the unemployed and the excluded, but they do not provide, by themselves, a lasting solution. While there is no question of abandoning income-redistribution policies, it is the income distribution which is inherent to the mode of production that should be the primary focus of our attention.

Beyond measures relating to employment, it is urgent to provide the dispossessed and marginalized populations with the means by which they can more efficiently claim their rights. To achieve this goal, it is necessary to promote education for citizenhood,[30] namely to:

- raise the consciousness of all populations (children, young people and adults) and notably of groups discriminated against

[29] In this respect, see the books by Johnson, Chalmers (1982), Sautter, Christian (1987) and Wade, Robert (1990), the already cited articles by Deepak Nayyar and Lance Taylor and the presentation by Robert Delorme (1995) of the approach put forward by the so-called evolutionary economics school.

[30] The search for new forms of education for citizenhood and of the learning of social roles from the primary school stage are additions to the many, so-to-speak classical functions of education and training in development strategies. See the already mentioned document by the Director-General of UNESCO prepared for the Copenhagen Summit (cf. Note 6).

(women, children, when applicable cultural minorities) about their rights and duties;

– train them as regards action they can take when their rights are not respected or violated: how to get organized, where to look for effective aid, whom to call on at the practical and moral levels, how to mobilize public opinion.

At the same time, to ensure real, day-to-day participation by populations in the decision-making and management process, it is necessary to carry out an indepth analysis of the institutional context and of the relationships among the social actors concerned, namely the organized civil society (citizens' association and social movements), the social economy, government authorities at all levels and the world of enterprise. Special attention has to be paid to:

– institutions that play a mediating role between the populations and the State beyond those of representative democracy alone (ombudsmen, forums and consultative councils, advocacy planning, forms of institutionalized cooperation between governmental bodies and citizens' associations);

– the practices of direct democracy (referenda, opinion polls, interactive media);

– positive discrimination policies (and their often perverse effects).

New Forms of Partnership among the Social Actors

Participation plays a major role in the rhetoric of development. However, the reality often takes the form of strategies elaborated at the central level and imposed from above. It is necessary to rehabilitate the opposite approach favouring bottom-up initiatives, notably as regards the identification of the real needs of the population and of their hierarchy in terms of urgency.[31] This means

---

[31] This brings us back to the debate on 'basic needs', their weak version determined by the authorities and their strong version when it is the concerned parties that establish the hierarchy of these needs. In this respect, see Wisner, B. (1988) and the fundamental contribution by Sen, A. K. (1986) to the theory of the satisfaction of needs showing the multiplicity of forms that could come into play (entitlements).

strengthening the ability of the populations to assume responsibility for a large part of the decisions that concern them, in a word, their *empowerment*. Two dangers however need to be avoided.

Firstly, there are manipulated ambiguities around this concept. John Friedmann (1992) has rightly made empowerment the cornerstone of the search for alternative development strategies. However, it should not be forgotten that this very same word was frequently uttered by President Reagan and, coming from him, it meant that the State was giving up certain of its responsibilities and passing them on to the local government institutions. A weak interpretation of the concept lies at the basis of the community programme proposed by A. Etzioni (1993). The same type of ambiguity hovers over the concept of subsidiarity cherished by the European Commission. A decision that can be taken at a lower level ought not to go up to the upper level. But then the question is who is to take a decision on this point.

Furthermore, it would be vain to expect that the complexity of today's world would make it possible for us to be satisfied with a mere juxtaposition of a multitude of local strategies. The linkages among the spaces of development, from the local to the regional, national and transnational levels, constitute a major area of concern for political action. The present imbalance in favour of the central level and its incapacity to think out strategies that are finely tuned to local contexts makes it necessary to encourage initiatives from the bottom. And yet, such initiatives need to be harmonized and assisted by making available to them critically necessary resources that cannot be mobilized on the spot.

In other words, public policies and citizens' actions need to be harmonized. This major theme for the Social Summit was debated in the International Conference on Public Policies, People's Actions and Social Development organized by UNESCO in December 1994 in collaboration with the City and University of Bologna. The conference reviewed several specific examples of the linkage between citizens' movements and State policies, notably the programme of the fight against hunger and for citizenship in Brazil,[32] the solidarity programme in Mexico, the role of citizens'

---

[32] One of the first measures taken by Brazil's new President, Fernando Henrique Cardoso, was to set up an ambitious programme called 'Solidarity Community' based on the principle of partnership between the State and citizens' movements.

organizations in the struggle against exclusion in Poland. It also discussed the prospects ahead following the end of apartheid in South Africa and European research on the reform of Welfare States, with a view to establishing a 'caring society'[33] through partnership among the parties concerned. The development of the social, educational and health services, as well as of the services related to making use of the time released from work, provides a vast field for the setting up of new structures of partnership among users, citizens associations, local government authorities and private firms.

This area is a particularly promising one for the countries of the South and the East where the general level of wages is presently low. Indeed, since the 'productivity' of teachers, nurses or social workers is approximately the same in every country in the world, in absolute terms the cost of producing such services in these countries is low in comparison with their cost in countries where the average level of salaries is high. With a slight modification at the margin of allocation of resources to social services in the broad sense of the term, it would therefore be possible to obtain a substantial improvement in the quality of life in the poor countries. Instead of awaiting prosperity in order to begin developing social services, it is necessary on the contrary to hasten to do so immediately.

The final Round Table in Bologna was devoted to urban experiments in Italy. It showed the wealth, variety and scale of the concrete experiments carried out at the municipal level. The cities whose almost infinite diversity has been so well brought out by Italo Calvino (1974) are indeed the crucible for the emergence and shaping of new forms of citizenhood. In this field, Italy has been a stupendous laboratory for centuries. The development of urban citizenhood will be necessary if we truly wish to make our cities liveable in the twenty-first century. This goal will not be a greater

---

[33] In this respect, see the study by Laura Balbo presented at Bologna (see Note 8), the recent work by Pierre Rosanvallon (1995), and for the antecedents of these debates, the study prepared by the Secretariat of Future Studies in Sweden (Lägergren, M., et al., 1984). The growth of the third sector in the world has been the subject of a set of reports organized by Civicus, World Alliance for the Participation of Citizens (see for Latin America, Rubem Cesar Fernandes, 1994 and for Eastern Europe, E. Les, 1994).

burden on our economies, especially in the industrial countries, than the construction of cathedrals were in the Middle Ages. The urban crisis needs to be treated on a priority basis. It is also in the urban framework that the questions of inter-ethnic, inter-cultural and inter-religious relationships are being raised. These issues are a source of numerous conflicts and endemic violence, especially in situations where the mixing of different social and cultural groups is overlaid on a context of social exclusion.[34]

Science and Technology in the Service of Social Development

Technology is a key variable for the bringing of social, economic and environmental policies into harmony. The question is whether it is conceivable to put a brake on the present dominant trend in which technological progress means jobless growth and the role that could be played in this field by the reorientation of scientific research.

This question was put to researchers at the International Conference of Science and Technology for Social Development organized in Delhi in December 1994 by UNESCO and the National Institute for Science, Technology and Development Studies (NISTADS). They were asked in particular what was the potential contribution by science and technology to the three aspects of an alternative development strategy centred on the exploration of three sources of employment which are briefly described here below:

1. The working of economies is presently characterized by the wasting, in varying degrees, of energy, water and other natural resources. Considerable progress remains to be made in the recycling of wastes and materials. Moreover, a more methodical maintenance of equipment, infrastructures and installations that would prolong their useful life is one way of saving capital. These activities, which are major sources of job-creation, are self-financing, at least partly so, through the saving of physical resources and of capital that they bring about.

2. In rural areas, the decisive battle for jobs will be fought around the future of the small farms. The small farm is destined

---

[34] The UNESCO programme on the 'Management of Social Transformations' (MOST) concentrates its activities of research and of proposing new policies specifically on these questions.

to disappear in the long term, if we extrapolate from the presently observed dominant trends of technical progress in agriculture. However, provided that it is properly managed, the new phase of the green revolution makes it possible to envisage the modernization of agriculture for the benefit of the small farmer. It may be added that a better use of available agricultural land is in the interest also of the industrialized countries, inasmuch as they might wish to avoid being turned into urban archipelagos in a rural desert.

Furthermore, efforts should also be made to create non-agricultural rural jobs, which can be obtained in two ways:

 – through the growth of biomass-transforming agro-industries and through the substitution of fossil fuel energy by bio-energy;
 – through the redeployment of industries and tertiary activities, made possible by advances in telecommunications and the growing importance of flexible specialization.

3. Finally, we must mention the classic case of public works where technical choices are not dictated by international competition. The needs in terms of infrastructure are especially urgent in countries whose systemic competitivity leaves much to be desired. So long as this competitivity has not been improved, piecemeal investments to increase productivity in firms will, to a large extent, be lost.

The discussions in Delhi concentrated largely on the first two aspects. The papers presented by the participants showed the importance attached in the world's two most populous countries (China and India) to the devising of development strategies heavily geared to the creation of rural jobs, both agricultural and industrial, and also characterized by the saving of scarce resources such as agricultural soil and water. In both cases, the goal is, as far as possible, to reduce country–city migrations. Hyper-urbanization, as in Latin America, would lead to an economic, social and ecological disaster.

A great many Indian studies, as well as field experiments undertaken (for example, ASTRA at Indian Institute of Science, Bangalore, the Swaminathan Foundation in Madras and Development Alternatives in Delhi), have shown that it is possible to use biotechnologies in very small family farms,[35] to design integrated village systems for the production of food and energy from the biomass[36] and to create industrial jobs in the countryside with exceedingly low investment and reasonable productivity. The pioneering experiments, as yet small in number, carried out by Development Alternatives have resulted in the creation of sustainable jobs in small companies, dam construction work and soil and water management requiring, in certain cases, barely $ 200 to $ 300 per job created.

The Chinese programme SPARK for the spreading of modern science and technology in a rural environment has, according to the paper presented by its representative, already helped create one hundred million non-agricultural rural jobs. Ashok Jain, Director of NISTADS presented a very fine analysis of the prospects for decentralized modern industrialization in India in the light of the experience of the *terza Italia*.[37]

The importance of the Delhi meeting lies in the fact that it has shown the existence of a current of thought and action that runs counter to the dominant tendency. This enables a certain degree of equanimity to be maintained when contemplating the extremely complex challenges that face the densely populated countries of the South. This message can be clearly seen in a major collective work on science, population and development organized by V. Gowariker (1992), suggestively entitled *The Inevitable Billion Plus*.

The condition of success is that research in the countries of the South should not be made subservient to the dominant modes in the laboratories of the North and that there should be no passive waiting for the transfer of technologies developed in other latitudes and other contexts. The ambition to leapfrog the industrial

[35] On the prospects and dangers of the biotechnological revolution for the countries of the South, see notably, *Biotechnology Revolution and the Third World* (1988), Ahmed (1992) and Sasson (1993).

[36] On this subject see Moulik (1988) and Sachs and Silk (1990).

[37] For an analysis of the determinants of the success of the Italian experience in decentralized modern industrialization, which has brought wealth to northeast Italy, see notably Bagnasco (1988), Pyke, Beccatini and Sengenberger (1990) and Pyke and Sengenberger (1992). Trigilia (1992) examines the reasons for the failure of the mimetic transposition of this model to southern Italy.

countries in certain fields of research is quite legitimate. This is why it is the strengthening of local capacity in terms of science, technology and the training of highly qualified cadres that is the essential feature of development strategies based on the ability to think independently and carry out national projects.

The authors of the already mentioned report of the International Commission for Peace and Food, consider as viable a strategy to provide a billion new jobs in the countries of the South within barely 10 years (pp. 198–9). This proposal generalizes from the results of a study proposing to achieve full employment in India in one decade, thus raising the entire Indian population above the poverty threshold (op. cit. pp. 122–4). To achieve this end, it would be necessary to create 100 million new jobs, including 15 million in agriculture, 10 million in rural agro-industries and 45 million rural and urban jobs due to the multiplier effect of increased consumption by the rural masses, agriculture being both a source of food and biomass and an outlet for industrial products and services. According to the authors of this strategy, the country could achieve this spectacular result without resorting to external resources other than direct investment by agro-industrial firms. The condition for this, however, is that the country should be able to export its agricultural surpluses without any hindrance of its access to the markets of the industrial countries. The report therefore sharply criticizes the agricultural protectionism of the developed countries and suggests a world strategy of development of the South through the expansion of its agricultural or forestry exports. At present, 58 per cent of the economically active population in the countries of the South, namely 1.1 billion men, women and children, work in agriculture whereas there are only 35 million working in this sector in the industrial countries. This entire reasoning is based on a controversial assessment of the potential of agriculture for the future. According to the authors of the report, the availability of soil and water for agriculture could easily be doubled at the planetary level and productivity per hectare could also be very considerably increased.

What may be retained from this surprisingly optimistic exercise is above all the idea that, contrary to a very widespread prejudice, agriculture could be an engine of growth in development, at least in certain countries of Asia, Africa and Latin America, provided that the efforts are concentrated on labour-intensive crops and on a careful management of soil, micronutrients and water using knowledge-intensive techniques.

A complement of this strategy consists in exploring biodiversity and cultural diversity to find new resources and manage them in a socially useful and ecologically prudent way so as to increase the capacity of the ecosystems on a lasting basis. This requires making simultaneous use of knowledge accumulated by populations and of the conquests of modern science.[38]

Reforms of the International System

This analysis would be incomplete without mentioning the need to rethink the working of the UN system and of the Bretton Woods[39] institutions to create an international environment that is more propitious to development, notably by recalling the fact that equity in international relations requires that the rules of the game should be biased in favour of the weaker partners. This principle was complied with when the UNCTAD was created. Will this be true also for the future World Trade Organization?

What can be done to give social movements and citizens' associations a more active role, than the one they presently have, in the working of the major international organizations? In the context of the Copenhagen Conference, two aspects of this question need to be raised. Firstly, these associations could take on the responsibility of preparing citizens' reports on the world's social condition, following the example of what was done for the environment in India. Secondly, it is necessary to think about the creation of an institution enjoying unquestionable moral authority, to which citizens' organizations could appeal, thereby alerting public opinion about violations of political, civic, social, cultural and economic rights and thus influencing the functioning of governmental and intergovernmental institutions.

---

[38] This goal is being pursued by the UNESCO South–South Co-operation programme for environmentally sound socio-economic development in the humid tropics.

[39] On this subject see notably Holland (1994).

References

Ahmed, I. (ed.) (1992), *Biotechnology. A Hope or a Threat?* A Study Prepared for the International Labour Office within the Framework of the World Employment Programme, The Macmillan Press Ltd., Londres.

Aznar, G. (1993), *Travailler moins pour travailler tous*, Syros, Paris.

Badie, B. (1994), *Nouvel Ordre ou Nouveau Désordre Mondial*, Cercle Condorcet, Les Points de Vue n° 13, November, Paris.

Badie, B. et Smouts, M. C. (1992), *Le retournement du monde*, Presses de la Fondation Nationale des Sciences Politiques, Dalloz, Paris.

Bagnasco, A. (1988), *La Construzzione Sociale del Mercato*, Il Mulino, Bologna.

Bartoli, H. (1991), *L'économie multidimensionnelle*, Economica, Paris.

Belorgey, J. M. (1994), 'Evaluation de la politique de la ville', *Hommes, Libertés et territoires*, February–March.

Biotechnology Revolution and The Third World. Challenges and Policy Options, (1988), Research and Information System for the Non-Aligned and Other Developing Countries (RIS), New Delhi.

Brunetta, R. (1994), *La fine della società dei salariati*, I. Grilli Marsilio, Venice.

Brunhes, B. (1993), Interview, in Mazel, O., *Les chômages*, Le Monde éditions, p. 169, Paris.

Calvino, I. (1974), *Les villes invisibles*, Le Seuil, Paris.

Castel, R. (1995), *Les métamorphoses de la question sociale—une chronique on salariat*, Fayard, Paris.

Comeliau, Ch. (ed.) (1994), *Ingérence économique. La mécanique de la soumission*, Les Nouveaux Cahiers de l'Institut Universitaire d'Etudes du Développement de Genève, Preses Universitaires de France, Paris.

Delorme, R. (1995), 'An Evolutionary Theoretical Framework for the State–Economy Interactions in Transforming Economies'. Contribution to the Round Table on the Forms of Organization and Transformations in the Economies of Central and Eastern Europe, Paris, 26–7 January.

Dessus, B. (1995), *Systèmes énergétiques pour un développement durable*, (Ph. D thesis in Applied Economics), University Pierre Mendès France, Grenoble.

Dollfus, O. (1994), *L'Espace Monde*, Economica, Paris.

Drucker, P. F. (1986), 'The Changed World Economy', *Foreign Affairs*, pp. 768–91.

Echange et Projets (1980), *La révolution du temps choisi,* Albin Michel, Paris.

Economie et Humanisme (1986), *Louis-Joseph Lebret; regards 86,* Lyon.

Ehrlich, Paul R. and H. Anne (1990), *The Population Explosion,* Simon and Schuster, New York.

Emmerij, L. (1994), 'Tensions sociales et réforme sociale en Amérique Latine', Communication to the International Forum on Latin American Perspectives, organized by IDB and OECD Development Centre, Paris, 2–4 November.

Etzioni, A., (1993), *The Spirit of Community. Rights, Responsibilities, and the Communitarian Agenda,* Crown Publishers, New York.

Friedmann, J. (1992), *Empowerment—The Politics of Alternative Development,* Blackwell, Cambridge, Mass. and Oxford, UK.

Goldemberg, J., Reddy, A. K., Williams R. et Johansson, Th., (1988), *Energy for a Sustainable World,* Wiley Eastern Limited, New Delhi.

Gorz, A. (1988), *Métamorphoses du travail: quéte du sens,* Galilée, Paris.

Gowariker, V. (ed.) (1992), *The Inevitable Billion Plus. Science, Population and Development,* Unmesh Communications, Pune.

Group of Lisbon, The (R. Petrella et al.) (1993), *Limits to Competition,* Gulbenkian Foundation, Lisbon.

Hausner, J. (1994), *Negotiated in the Transformation of Post-Socialist Economy.* Cracow Academy of Economics, Cracow.

Holand, S. (1994), *Towards a New Bretton Woods. Alternatives or the Global Economy,* Spokesman, Nottingham.

Illich, I. (1977), *Le chômage créateur. Postface à la convivialité,* Le Seuil, Paris.

ILO (1986), *Population Active 1950–2025,* vol. 5 (Monde résumé), Geneva.

International Commission on Peace and Food (Chaired by M. S. Swaminathan) (1994), *Uncommon Opportunities. An Agenda for Peace and Equitable Development,* Zed Books, London and New Jersey.

Jean-Paul II (1994), *Questions sociales. Travail—Développement—Economie,* Librairie Générale Francaise, Paris.

Johnson, Chalmers (1982), *MITI and the Japanese Miracle,* Stanford University Press, Stanford.

Keynes, J. M. (1972), 'Economic Possibilities for our Grandchildren' in *The Collected Writings, vol. IX, Essays in Persuasion,* Macmillan, London.

Kothari, R. (1993), *Growing Amnesia. An Essay on Poverty and the Human Consciousness,* Viking/Penguin Books, New Delhi.

Krugman, P. (1994), *Peddling Prosperity,* W. W. Norton, New York.

Kula, W., (1960), 'Secteurs et régions arriérés dans l'économic du capitalisme naissant', *Studi Storici*, n° 3.

Leadbeater, Ch. and Lloyd, J. (1987), *In Search of Work*, Penguin Books, Harmondsworth.

Les, E. (1994), *The Voluntary Sector in Post-Communist East Central Europe. From Small Circles of Freedom to Civil Society*, Civicus, Washington.

Maddison, A. (1994), 'Monitoring the World Economy 1820–1992', OECD Development Centre, Paris.

Meade, J. (1986), *Different Forms of Share Economy*, Public Policy Centre, London.

———— (1989), *Agathotopia. L'economia della partnership*, Feltrinelli, Milano.

Morin, E. et Kern, A. B. (1993), *Terre-Patrie*, Editions due Senil, Paris.

Moulik, T. K. (ed.) (1988), *Food-Energy Nexus and Ecosystem*, Proceedings of the Second International Symposium on Food-Energy Nexus and Ecosystem held in New Delhi, India (12–14 February 1986), Mohan Primlani for Oxford & IBH Publishing, New Delhi.

Naisbitt, J. (1995), *Global Paradox*, Avon Books, New York.

Nayyar, D. (1993), *The Indian Economy at Crossroads: Illusions and Realities*, Frontier Lecture of the Jawaharlal Nehru Centre for Advanced Scientific Research and the Indian Institute of Science, Bangalore, 25 February.

Ortiz, R. (1994), *Mundializasão e Cultura*, Editora Brasiliense, São Paulo.

Petrella, R. (1994), 'Litanies de Sainte Compétitivité', *Le Monde diplomatique*, Manière de Voir 22 (May), Paris.

Pyke, F. and Sengenberger, W. (eds) 1992, *Industrial Districts and Local Economic Regeneration*, International Institute for Labour Studies, Geneva.

Pyke, F., Becattini, G. and Sengenberger, W. (eds) (1990), *Industrial Districts and Inter-Firm Co-operation in Italy*, International Institute for Labour Studies, Geneva.

Rahman Khan, A. (1993), *Structural Adjustment and Income Distribution. Issues and Experiences*, ILO, Geneva.

Ramonet, I. (1994), 'Un horizon d'espoir', *Le Monde Diplomatique*, Manière de voir, n° 22, May, Paris.

Reich, R. (1992), *The Work of Nations. Preparing Ourselves for 21st Century Capitalism*, Vintage Books, New York.

Riboud, A. (1987), *Modernization, mode d'emploi*, Union générale d'édition, Paris.

Rigaudiat, J. (1993), *Réduire le temps de travail*, Syros, Paris.

Rosanvallon, P. (1995), *La nouvelle question sociale. Repenser l'Etat-providence*, Le Seuil, Paris.

Ruffolo, G. (1988), *Potenza e Potere. La fluttuazione gigante dell'Occidente*, Laterza, Bari.

Sachs, I. (1980), 'Les temps-espaces du développement', *Diogène*, n° 112, pp. 80–95.

———— (1984), *Development and Planning*, transl. by P. Fawcett, Cambridge University Press, Cambridge; New York and New Rochelle.

———— (1990) (in collaboration with D. Silk), *Food and Energy: Strategies for Sustainable Development*, United Nations University Press, Tokyo, p. 83.

———— (1993), *Eco-development. Strategies of Transition towards the 21st Century*, Interest Publications, New Delhi.

———— (1993), 'Population, Development and Employment', *International Social Science Journal*, no. 141, pp. 343–59.

Saint-Geours, J. (1992), *Moi et nous. Politique de la société mixte*, Dunod, Paris.

Salomon, J. J. (1984), *Prométhée empétro—résistance au changement technique*, Editions Anthropos, Paris.

———— (1992), *Le destin technologique*, Balland, Paris.

Salomon, J. J., Sagasti, F. et Sachs-Jeantet, C. (eds) (1994), *The Uncertain Quest—Science, Technology, and Development*, United University Press Tokyo.

Sasson, A. (1993), *Biotechnologies in Developing Countries: Present and Future*, vol. 1, UNESCO, Paris, p. 164.

Sautter, Ch. (1987), *Les denis du dragon*, Orban, Paris.

Sen, A. K. (1986), *Food, Economics and Entitlements*, WIDER Working Paper 1, Helsinki.

———— (1987), *On Ethics and Economics*, Basil Blackwell, Oxford.

———— (1992), *Inequality Reexamined*, Harvard University Press, Cambridge, Mass.

Sengenberger, W., Loveman, G. W. and Piore, M. J. (1990), *The Reemergence of Small Enterprises: Industrial Restructuring in Industrialized Countries*, International Institute for Labour Studies, Geneva.

Serres, M. (1990), *Le contrat naturel*, Francois Bourin, Paris.

Streeten, P. (1989), *Mobilizing Human Potential. The Challenge of Unemployment*, UNDP Policy Discussion Paper, UNDP, New York.

Taylor, L. (1994), 'Economic Reform: India and Elsewhere', *Economic and Political Weekly*, 20 August.

Time to Care. Politiche del tempo e diritti quotidiani (1987), a cura di Laura Balbo, Franco Angeli, Milan.

Trigilia, C. (1992), *Sviluppo Senza Autonomia. Effetti perversi delle politiche nel Mezzogiorno*, Il Mulino, Bologna.

Tsuru, S. (1993), *Japan's Capitalism: Creative Defeat and Beyond*, Cambridge University Press, Cambridge.

UNDP (1994), *World Report on Human Development 1994*.

Wade, Robert (1990), *Governing the Market: Economic Theory and the Role of Government in East Asian Industrialization*, Princeton University Press, Princeton.

Weitzman, M. L. (1985), *L'economia della partecipazione*, Laterza, Bari.

'What Now?' (1975), Dag Hammarskjöld Report on Development and International Cooperation, *Development Dialogue*, nr. 1/2.

Wisner, B. (1988), *Power and Need in Africa*, Earthscan Publications Limited, London.

Wolfe, M. (1994), 'Some Paradoxes of Social Exclusion', International Institute for Labour Studies, Discussion paper 63/1994, Geneva.

2

Social Sustainability and Whole Development

In the aftermath of the 1992 Earth Summit the adjective 'sustainable' became a must in the rhetoric of national and international politics, both in the South and in the North. A lot of semantic confusion has arisen from the loose use of this word, to which different people attach different meanings.

Complaining about such abusive practices during the Istanbul Habitat II, David Satterwhaite (1996) pointed out that the real issues are not 'sustainable cities' (what does it mean exactly?) but 'sustainable patterns of production and consumption' Even among those proponents of 'sustainable cities' who recognize the urgency of meeting urban human needs in a better way 'there is little agreement over what is to be sustained—livelihoods, development projects, policies, institutions, businesses, the city, culture or economic growth' (p. 32).

As for the concept of 'social sustainability', also raised in Istanbul, the ambiguity was whether it meant the social preconditions for sustainable development or the need to sustain specific social structures and customs. Major transformations of these structures and a questioning of the present distribution of power are likely to appear as preconditions to sustainable development. This appears clearly when one addresses the central question—why are so many people's needs not being met today?—moving to the analysis of economic, social and political causes of unemployment, poverty and social exclusion.

This essay attempts at reflecting on social sustainability from the perspective of development studies understood as a 'field' (or a 'problematique') cutting across several traditionally defined social sciences and prefiguring perhaps a unified 'eco-social-political economy'.[1]

Sustainability evokes steadiness, a combination of regularity and perennity.[2] In its present form, the debate on sustainability in general and social sustainability in particular, can be traced back to the 'environmental revolution' of the sixties brought about by a conjunction of factors:

  – the realization of the finiteness of our planet, a somewhat paradoxical reaction to a major technical feat– the landing on the moon.

  – the dangers inherent to the Faustian bargain associated with the nuclear race and, more generally, with the impossibility of finding a shortcut to development through quick technological fixes (see Salomon, Sagasti, Sachs-Jeantet (eds), 1994).

  – the recurring Malthusian spectre of mismatch between an exponentially growing population (these were the years of baby boom), specially in the poor South, and the limited stock of agricultural land and natural resources.

  – last, but not the least, the environmental disruption provoked by the rapid economic growth of the fifties and sixties (Sachs, 1994b).

A decade earlier, an economic historian, W. Rostow (1960) put into circulation the concept of 'self-sustained growth' with no relation whatsoever to environment. Rostow's grand theory (which he himself termed a 'non-communist Manifesto') was meant as a substitute for Marx's historical materialism. According to Rostow, the developing countries should not think about anti-capitalist revolutions. Once they go through a successful take-off and give themselves the necessary institutional setting to promote private accumulation, they will enter on the orbit of a continuous process

---

[1] See on this point Kapp, W. (1987).

[2] cf. Costanza, R. and B. C. Patten, (1995): 'The basic idea of sustainability is quite straightforward: a sustainable system is one which survives or persists', (p. 193).

of growth, repeating the successful path pioneered by the developed countries of today. Rostow's book was presented as a major intellectual breakthrough by cold war propaganda. But it fell rapidly into oblivion and we need not to be concerned with it in this essay.

The debate between the doomsayers (apocalypse tomorrow by exhaustion of resources and/or by asphyxia from pollution) and the cornucopians (exponential growth of GNP extrapolated into centuries to come), was initially concerned with the physical limits of the increase of material output.[3] But soon it became clear that besides these 'outer' limits, it was also necessary to consider the 'inner' limits inherent in human societies.

Unlike other organisms, humankind lives, for better or for worse, in two environments—a physical one and a symbolic, non-material, cultural one, which is the product of his own activity. We need not, at this stage, take position with respect to Anatol Rapoport's (1974) anguishing query: 'It is a moot question whether this new and unique kind of dependence enhances or jeopardizes the long-term survival potential of the human species' (p. 45).[4]

Whatever the reply, social sustainability appears as a concern related to the internal organization of each human society and of

[3] More precisely, one should speak of 'throughput' as waste disposal is part of the picture and nature is put to contribution at both ends of the production process, as 'source' (natural capital) and 'sink' (environmental resilience).

[4] For Rapoport, man's interaction with the physical environment differs only quantitatively, not qualitatively, from corresponding interactions of other animals: 'A house is but an elaborate nest. A super-highway is an improved cow-path. A hydroelectric dam is like a beaver dam magnified manifold. A fishing net is analogous to a spider web.

The other environment, the symbolic one, has no real analogue in the non-human world. There are no precursors among animals of epic poems, monuments, preferred stock, protest marches, confessions, astronomy, or astrology' (p. 51).

Two qualifications are in order here. Firstly, the scale of human intervention, in contrast with that of animals, has become so large as to interfere with the working of the biosphere. Secondly, we live in three environments, a natural environment more or less modified by human action, the socio-cultural environment and, last but not least, a man-made artificial environment of which the spaceship is the most extreme example. Cities combine the three in a variety of environments, perceived in diverse ways by different groups of people (environment is always related to a subject).

the world community of increasingly interdependent[5] nations, taken as a whole.

Absence of war, of major violence and of social anomie and a non-totalitarian political regime are the main ingredients of a weak definition of social sustainability. We ought to be more demanding. As D. Goulet (1995) puts it:

...ethical agendas are predicated not on accepting things as they are, but on struggling to make them what they ought to be: to create new possibilities is the supreme moral imperative (p. 180).

A strong definition of social sustainability must rest on the foundational values of equity and democracy, the latter meant as the effective appropriation of all the human rights—political, civil, economic, social and cultural—by all the people (see Sachs, 1995b). Adopting A. Sen's focus on human capabilities, a sustainable society should continuously enhance peoples' ability to do and be what they have reason to value (Sen, A. 1985, 1987 and 1996).[6]

For that, it is necessary to transcend the economic solipsism, as postulated by Karl Polanyi (1977):

What should be the end of man, and how should he choose his means? Economic rationalism, in the strict sense, has no answer to these questions, for they imply motivations and valuations of a moral and practical order that go beyond the irresistible but otherwise empty, exhortation to be 'economical' (p. 13).[7]

A key ethical question which the affluent minority must consider is: how much is enough?[8] Can conspicuous consumption be downtailed by self-restraint postulated by Gandhi? This question may seem odd. Yet peaceful changes in lifestyles, indispensable if we want to achieve sustainability, depend on our ability to cope with it.

[5] Interdependence encompasses different sorts of relations from symbiosis to parasitism, from mutually beneficial and symmetrical ('co-development') to asymmetrical and irreversible domination.

[6] cd. J. L. Lebret's concept of a civilization of being in an equitable sharing of having (de l'être dans le partage équitable de l'avoir).

[7] Robert Heilbroner (1993, p. 151) pursues a similar idea when, examining the prospect for the twenty-first century, he redefines 'socialism' as a society disconnected from the very idea of economic determinism.

[8] For an interesting debate on this question in Sweden consult 'What Now?' (1975).

As emphasized in Cocoyoc Declaration[9], it is maldistribution and not scarcity that lies at the root of the problem. Underconsumption and overconsumption, underdevelopment and overdevelopment are two sides of the same coin. Those who preempt over 75 per cent of all available resources must moderate their appetites and make room for those whose basic needs are not met.

At the same time, the development ethics must be broadened, so as to include environmental wisdom: 'there can be no social development ethics without environmental wisdom and, conversely, no environmental wisdom without a social development ethic' (Goulet, op. cit. p. 119).

[9] In the intellectual journey which started with the Founex Seminar on Environment and Development in 1991 and led in 1972 to Stockholm Conference on Human Development up to the Rio Earth Summit in 1992, the Cocoyoc Symposium has a very special place. It was convened from 8 to 12 October 1974 by UNEP and UNCTAD to discuss resource-use patterns in the context of environment and development and was chaired by Barbara Ward. The President of Mexico joined the seminar on the last day and fully supported the declaration, a strongly worded manifesto for a human-centred and need-oriented development. The anti-market bias of the declaration and its strongly worded radicalism were criticized by the American diplomacy. It took several years for UNEP to come back through a series of regional seminars to one of the main recommendations of Cocoyoc: the need to promote alternative lifestyles and development patterns (see UNEP, 1980). Yet the message of Cocoyoc was refined and consolidated in a report commissioned by the Dag Hammarskjöld Foundation ('What Now?,' 1975) built around the five pillars of 'another development': self-reliant, endogenous, need (and not demand) oriented, in harmony with nature and open to institutional change. Soon after the newly created International Foundation for Development Alternatives, operating from Nyon in Switzerland, started its 'third-system project' on the emergence of the civil society. Marc Nerfin, who directed the Dag Hammarskjöld Foundation project and presided the IFDA presented the main findings of the Third System project in a celebrated article: 'Neither Prince, nor Merchant: the Citizen—An Introduction to the Third System' (1986).

For a recent fairly accurate analysis of these developments, as well as of the elaboration of the eco-development concept started in Stockholm (see Sachs, 1974) consult Brohman, J. (1996 pp. 201–8 and pp. 307–10). However, Brohman presents 'another development' and 'eco-development' as independent endeavours, while they are closely associated. 'Another development' is but a further elaboration of eco-development and the third system project unfolded from them.

Such an ethic should explicitly assume the responsibility of human societies in protecting biodiversity and nurturing nature as part of co-evolution of the sociosphere and biosphere in which natural history and human history have been tightly interwoven.[10] The right to a healthy and pleasant environment should be likewise incorporated to the compact of human rights. But there is no reason to promote a separate Earth Charter, however commendable its substance (see Rockefeller, S. C., 1996) dispersing in this way the efforts that should all converge to consolidate the human rights compact. The more so that normative statements represent the easy part of the game, the real difficulty lies in their enforcement—'ecological morality, which controls practical interaction with nature, remains oddly unimpressed by ecological reason' (Eder, K., 1996, p. VII).

Insofar as social and environmental sustainability condition each other,[11] we are confronted by the double ethical imperative of synchronic and diachronic solidarity with the present and future generations and, as a corollary, invited to supplement the social contract by a natural contract (Serres, M., 1990).

The above stance posits a game with nature, not a game against it. It may, therefore, be viewed as an anthropocentric attitude tempered by the sense of responsibility for the future of the biosphere. It stops short of the Gaia principle. It also contradicts the stance taken by the deep ecologists. Humane development associated with the notion of ascent[12] is its central concern and

[10] Modern ecology has abandoned the equilibrium model borrowed from economics to become a sort of macro-history of nature, made possible by the reconstitution of the history of climates over a period of 150 thousand years (see Botkin, 1990). Ironically, the historicization of ecology is occurring at a moment when mainstream economics accentuates its ahistorical stance.

[11] Social collapse, as the Russian example shows, has devastating environmental consequences. Conversely, environmental disruption becomes a social cost. But the symmetry is not complete because of different time-scales and of the irreversibility of certain ecological damages. Painful as it may be, reversal of social situations is almost always possible given the political determination.

[12] Notwithstanding the terrible balance of the twentieth century, mostly when seen from European perspective, with its two world wars, genocides, crematories, gulags and the collapse of 'real socialism', I find it difficult to write off completely the idea of progress inherited from enlightenment and to give up all hope in the betterment of human societies.

sustainability is deemed meaningful only in this context. Consequently, conservation of nature is always seen through the prism of the people living in its midst, with a view to establishing a symbiotic relationship between them and their environment. The myth of pristine nature ignores the interests of the forest people, who, more often than not, contribute by their action to the conservation or even enrichment of the biodiversity (Diegues, A., 1996). It is time to turn now to the concept of development.

From Economic Growth to 'Whole' Development

Development entered the international agenda after 1945, out of two concerns. These were the need to reconstruct the economies destroyed by the Second World War and to assist the emancipated former colonies.

The initial focus was to equate development with economic growth because countries were laying in ruins, the prevailing Zeitgeist was economistic and the reductionist theory known as *trickle down* was widely believed to work.[13] Once the economy was set in motion the rest would follow and the positive effects of growth would percolate to the bottom of social pyramid. But soon it became necessary to explicate other dimensions of development: social, cultural, political and, after 1972, *environmental* (sustainable).

Lastly, as a reaction to the reification of economics, it was deemed necessary to insist on the centrality of the development process and the importance of human capital.[14] Hence the UNDP reports on 'human development'.

[13] In a sense, this was a three-stage reductionism: from overall development to economic development, from economic development to economic growth, from economic growth to accumulation and investment, in tune with the mechanistic growth theories.

[14] 'Human capital', a misnomer, pushes the reification of people to its logical extreme. Why capital? The World Bank is working at present with four kinds of capital: the physical, the natural, the human and the social (see Serageldin, I. and A. Steer (eds) (1995) and 'Monitoring Environmental Progress', 1995). The new approach is welcome insofar as it departs from narrow 'economicism'. However, the Bank's economists seem unable to free themselves from the straightjacket of neoclassical paradigm which transforms everything that is not labour into different kinds of 'capital'. 'Social capital' is but

Economic, social, political, cultural, sustainable (ecologically), human.... How many more adjectives will be added to qualify development—a pluridimensional concept *par excellence*?

I venture to suggest that it would be better to agree on refraining from the use of these adjectives and, instead, providing a more thorough definition of development; or else to collapse them in the adjective 'whole' or 'total' by analogy with total history as practised by the school of *Annales*.[15] My preference for 'whole' is predicated on the following arguments:

– 'whole' denotes not only the manifold facets of development, but suggests that *all* the pertinent ones are taken into consideration;

– furthermore, it evokes the cybernetic concept of the 'whole' and the holistic (systemic) approaches;

– finally it makes a reference to Francois Perroux' concern with the development of the *whole* man and *all* men.[16]

Whatever the semantic preference, the important task is to explicate the content of the term development and its epistemological status.

Theories of economic growth usually adopt a reductionist mechanistic paradigm relating the growth of output to investment. Insofar as the world 'development' has been adapted from natural science, it may be tempting to give it an organistic interpretation. The parallel is however misleading. Organic development is entirely determined by the genetic character of the living organism and the interplay of environmental factors. It follows a rigid pattern: germination, growth, maturation, decay, decomposition.

By contrast, socio-economic development is an open-ended historical process which depends, at least in part, on human

---

a clumsy way of recognizing the importance of institutional factors. Moreover, they seem unable to reason in non-quantitative terms and, therefore, insist on estimating the value of different 'capitals' by making highly controversial assumptions and simplifications. Amartya Sen's boutade comes to mind in this connection: 'it is better to be vague and right than precise and wrong'.

[15] D. Goulet (op. cit.) uses the term 'integral authentic development'. Still another possibility would be 'global', but this word has now a special connotation in the context of the globalization processes.

[16] in French: *tout* l'homme et *tous* les hommes.

imagination, projects and decisions subject to the constraints of the natural environment and of the burden of the living past (history). Our species is the only one capable of inventing its future and of transforming its environment according to its will, hopefully tempered by the sense of realism and the principle of responsibility.

When we speak of the birth, ascent, decline and fall of nations, it is only in loose metaphoric terms. At most, the etymology of 'development' (removing the ball from the grain) suggests another metaphor equating development with liberation: liberation from want and liberation from oppression and man-made institutional fetters hampering development.

Thus, development may be understood as an intentional self-guided process of transformation and management of socio-economic structures, directed at ensuring to all people an opportunity to lead a full and rewarding life by providing them with decent livelihoods and by continuously improving their well-being, whatever the concrete content given to these goals by different societies in different periods of time.

It is a matter of discussion: how to evaluate the degree of success of development policies beyond such indicators as the income distribution, access to social services, life expectancy, health, etc. Happiness does not yield itself to be measured, except perhaps, as once suggested by Johan Galtung, by counting how many times per day people smile.

I am skeptical about the possibility of building a meaningful composite index of development and, even more, about the need for such an index. Newspapers have a penchant to rank countries using such indices, but it serves little practical purpose. The profile approach, worked out and then abandoned by United Nations Research Institute for Social Development (UNRISD), looked more promising.[17] There is no reason why we should not make use of a battery of indicators supplemented by qualitative information.

The more so that values, aspirations and life-styles belong to the realm of cultural diversity, which does not yield itself to statistical treatment. The cultural diversity of societies is compound by the even greater diversity of individual life-paths. Societies only create

[17] For a fuller discussion see the special number on Measuring and Evaluating Development, *International Social Science Journal* (UNESCO), no. 143, March, 1995.

opportunities or obstacles to individual development, which ultimately rests on a unique biographical component.

The Controversy on Growth

So far, development has been associated with the necessary, but not sufficient condition of economic growth. From the social point of view, the same growth rhythms may lead to development, maldevelopment or even de-development. The latter case happens when economic growth provokes a heterogeneization of the society with associated phenomena of social exclusion (Sachs, 1987, 1995a, 1996).

In the same way, growth can be environmentally benign or disruptive. In his very important book, first published in 1950, W. Kapp (1971) analysed environmental disruption as one of the many social costs externalized by the private enterprise in an unregulated market economy.[18]

Combining the three criteria—the economic, the social and the environmental—we may distinguish four types of economic growth:

– which is savage growth—socially inequitable and environmentally disruptive;

– socially benign but environmentally disruptive growth—of the kind we had in Europe from 1945 to 1975;

– environmentally benign but socially inequitable growth—a possible scenario for the future;

– finally, socially equitable and environmentally benign growth— the only one which corresponds in my understanding to the concept of development.

---

[18] For Kapp, the disruption of man's environment and the social costs resulting from productive activities were the most crucial problem faced by humanity, exceeded only in significance by the threat of nuclear holocaust. Conventional economic theory and national accounting were unable to cope theoretically and practically with this problem. A 'humanization of economic analysis' was therefore in order, together with new forms of social economic planning and decision making. Kapp, who considered himself an institutionalist, believed in the ultimate emergence of a unified social science. His book stands not only as a pioneering work, but also as a major landmark in the socio-economic literature on the environmental revolution.

This stance has been challenged by some environmental economists and, in particular, by Herman Daly (1990) who opposes
quantitative growth to qualitative development. For him, quantitative growth cannot be sustained in ecological terms, therefore,
sustainable growth is a 'bad oxymoron'. In economic terms,
development should rest as much as possible on renewable resources with harvest rates equal to regeneration rates. At the same
time, the waste emission rates should be kept equal to the natural
assimilative capacities of the ecosystems into which the wastes are
emitted.

Daly recognizes himself that this is a very stringent condition
which will make fighting poverty much more difficult. I find more
acceptable the position taken by the participants of the Asko
meeting (Arrow et al., 1995) insisting on the contents of growth
(and, I would say, on the uses of growth). It is totally unrealistic
to propose a meaningful strategy of poverty eradication in the
context of no growth; the qualitative aspects of development are
very important indeed but they are not a substitute for the material
satisfaction of some basic human needs. Even when postulating a
civilization of being, we should not forget that it requires as a
precondition an equitable sharing of having.

The real question, therefore, is to know how much time do we
have to implement a transition to a steady state? The doomsayers
claim that it is almost too late. Some epistemological optimists
consider that the progress of science will make it possible to
sustain growth for ever. I propose a middle path with a two stage
strategy.

The first phase, while paying attention to the environmental
aspects of growth, should concentrate its efforts on the eradication
of poverty and reduction of social inequalities within nations and
between nations. For this purpose, it should explore as much as
possible the 'three-win' opportunities for a socially equitable,
environmentally prudent and economically viable growth.[19] The
North should agree to moderate its conspicuous consumption

---

[19] Economic viability must be ascertained at the macro-social level taking
into account the environmental and social costs, not at the micro-entrepre-
neurial one where only profitability matters. In mixed economies, the aim of
economic policies is to create for the private enterprises a set of rules and
incentives that favours the 'three-win' solutions.

patterns and transfer resources massively to the South. The South should give up the idea that it could build equitable societies by imitating Northern development styles.[20]

The greater the degree of social equality achieved, the shorter will be the time-span required for this first transition phase. In a path-breaking study published in 1976, a team of Latin American scientists led by Amilcar Herrera demonstrated that in an egalitarian set-up the satisfaction of all basic needs in developing countries would require a GNP per capita three to five times lower than the one required if current income structures were maintained (Fundacion Bariloche, 1976). This goal could be achieved with moderate rates of growth on the condition of reducing the non-essential consumption. In Latin America, no more than 30 years would be needed. Another important conclusion of the study was that under prevailing conditions in most developing countries, increased foreign aid would have little or no effect on the living conditions of the majority of the population.

With the achievement of the first phase, the phasing out of material growth should become a more realistic proposition.

Partial Sustainabilities and Whole Sustainability

After this overview of the development field we may return to the question of sustainability introducing a distinction between partial sustainabilities and overall (whole) sustainability.[21] Insofar as development is a multidimensional, open-ended, evolutionary construct, to achieve a healthy genuine sustainable development, the sustainability criteria must be met in each pertinent dimension of development. We may thus speak of the need to meet the following criteria simultaneously.

– social sustainability and its corollary, cultural sustainability;

– ecological sustainability (conservation of the capital of nature) supplemented by the environmental and territorial sustainabilities, the former relative to the resilience of the natural ecosystems used as 'sinks', the latter evaluating the spatial

---

[20] For more details, see Sachs (1993).
[21] By analogy with Herbert Marcuse's treatment of rationality.

distribution of human activities and the rural–urban configura-tions;[22]

– economic sustainability taken in its broad meaning of effi-ciency of the economic systems (institutions, policies and rules of functioning) to ensure continuous socially equitable, quanti-tative and qualitative, progress.[23]

– last but not the least, political sustainability providing a satisfy-ing overall framework for national[24] and international gover-nance.

In our list social sustainability comes first, as it overlaps with the very finality of development. By contrast, economic and political sustainability are of an instrumental nature, while ecological sus-tainability occupies an intermediary position; it belongs to both the realms (finality and instrumentality).

A tentative list of criteria of partial sustainability is proposed in Table 2.1.

[22] I owe the distinction between ecological and environmental sustain-ability to Roberto P. Guimarães (1994). The territorial dimension of develop-ment is fundamental insofar as the same human activities have diverse social and environmental impacts depending on their location. As already men-tioned, maldistribution rather than scarcity is at the root of the present predicament of humanity. To be properly understood, social and environmen-tal problems require mapping, instead of misleading averages. The pioneering book, *Geography of Hunger*, published 50 years ago by Josué de Castro stands as a pointer.

[23] In a world plagued by massive unemployment and social exclusion, quantitative growth cannot be phased out. But its modalities, contents and uses must change so as to promote social, economic, and territorial sustainability while reducing, as much as possible, the negative ecological and environmental impacts.

[24] Given the collapse of the economies of command and the utopian character of the free market economy (a construct without real existence), we are left with the broad family of 'mixed economies' with diverse configurations of public and private sectors, the latter subdivided into profit-oriented enterprises and the 'social' or 'third' sector of citizen organization—cooperatives, associations, etc.—which are 'private yet public'. The different capitalisms, whatever the proposed classification (Albert, M. 1991), all belong to this category. An open question is whether 'social market economy' and 'market socialism' will converge.

TABLE 2.1

Criteria of Partial Sustainability

1. social	– achieving a fair degree of social homogeneity – equitable income distribution – full employment and/or self employment allowing the production of decent livelihoods – equitable access to resources and social services
2. cultural	– change within continuity (balance between respect of tradition and innovation) – capacity for autonomous design of a 'national project': self-reliance, endogeneity (as opposed to servile copying of alien models) and self-confidence, combined with an opening out to the world
3. ecological	– preserving the potential of 'natural capital' to produce renewable resources – limiting the use of depletable resources
4. environmental	– respecting and enhancing the capacity of natural ecosystems
5. territorial	– balanced rural–urban configurations (elimination of urban biases in the allocation of public investment) – enhancing urban environments – overcoming of inter-regional disparities – environmentally sound development strategies for ecologically fragile areas (conservation of biodiversity through eco-development)
6. economic	– balanced inter-sectoral economic development – food security – capacity to continuously modernize the production apparatus – fair degree of autonomy in Science and Technology research – sovereign insertion in the international economy
7. political (national)	– democracy defined in terms of universal appropriation of the whole human rights compact – a developmental State capable of implementing the national project in partnership with all the stakeholders – a fair degree of social cohesion

8. political (international) — effective UN system to prevent wars, protect peace and promote international cooperation
   — a North–South codevelopment compact based on the principle of equity (rules of the game and sharing of the burden biased in favour of the weaker partner)
   — effective institutional control of international finance and trade
   — effective institutional control of the application of the precautionary principle in the management of environment and natural resources, prevention of negative global change, protection of biological (and cultural) diversity and management of global commons as part of the common heritage of the humanity
   — effective international system of scientific and technological cooperation; partial decommoditization of Science and Technology as also belonging to the common heritage of humanity.

These criteria should be interpreted as indicating the desired direction of processes, rather than a final state; we are not in presence of a static zero-one situation (sustainability or lack of sustainability).

A few comments are in order here. In the real world the strong definition of whole sustainability must be relaxed, except as the projection of an ideal future, providing the overall perspective for long-term societal planning. It will be very difficult to meet simultaneously all the partial criteria or even to progress simultaneously along all the paths indicated by them. The real world is full of trade-offs. But this is no reason to be complacent about them. On the contrary, we ought to reject some trade-offs as clearly unacceptable while being prepared to tolerate for a limited period of time some others.

Thus, for example, whole development is incompatible with economic growth achieved through increased social inequality, and/or violation of democracy, even if its environmental impacts are kept under control. Environmental prudence, commendable as it is, cannot act as a substitute for social equity. Concern for the environment should not become a diversion from the paramount imperatives of social justice and full democracy, the two foundational values of whole development.

By contrast, we may partially relax the stringent criteria of ecological sustainability insofar as, for reasons already explained, economic growth tempered by ecological responsibility will remain, for decades to come, a necessary condition to achieve the 'social transition' to a steady state (defined by analogy with the demographic transition to a stationary population).

At any rate, in a world facing a major social crisis, with 30 per cent of the active population unemployed or severely underemployed, social exclusion on the rise, several hundred millions of people starving or chronically underfed, 600 million city dwellers living in appalling housing conditions and recurrent outbursts of local wars and genocide, the immediate danger comes from the violation of inner limits, even though the transgression of outer limits represents, in the longer run, a more insidious threat on account of its irreversibility and globality.

How long the affluent countries from the North will manage to insulate themselves from the consequences of the social catastrophes looming in the South is open for discussion. However, the divide between North and South goes beyond geography. Socially speaking, this divide opposes affluent nations and poor nations, but it also cuts across nations. We have a South in our countries, while the poor countries have an affluent elite which for all practical purposes is a Northern enclave.

From Concept to Action: Building and Sustaining Sustainability

Worldwide, the prevailing situation with few exceptions is characterized by a mix of maldevelopment and occasionally even development. Whole development appears at best a distant ideal.

To bridge the gap between the ideal and the present-day reality, it is suggested that the following three entry-points be used for the elaboration of the whole development agenda:

  – promotion of full employment and self-employment in conjunction with a more equitable sharing of work time (the latter being an element of a broader strategy, but by no means a panacea by itself); I submit that, contrary to the prevailing pessimism, full employment and self-employment remains a feasible and, what is more, indispensable goal within the social transition to a steady state;

– establishing an effective international regulation of the globalization processes with special reference to trade and finance;

– exploring alternative, resource-saving life-styles.

While the first and the second points are treated in subsequent chapters, an overview of the third one follows.

Changing Lifestyles

In 1993, Americans had one car per 1.8 inhabitants, in France, Germany and UK the ratio was of one car per 2.5 inhabitants. If the same level of motorization were to be reached in India and China,[25] another billion cars would have to be added to the present world total of some 500 million,[26] putting the carrying capacity of our planet to a very severe test.

Democratization of the individual motor car in the South is highly improbable and, most certainly, undesirable from the point of view of global environmental sustainability. The private car is likely to remain a positional good in a fragmented society distinguishing the privileged minority, at best the more prosperous half of the population, from the other half, and preempting the

---

[25] On the unlikely assumption that the two countries could cope with the infrastructural investment necessary to put on the roads the additional billion cars and with the hidden social costs of driving. These costs have been estimated for the United States by the World Resource Institute at 5.3 per cent of GDP, or better $ 2000 per year for each car, covering items such as building and repairing roads, loss of economic activity from congestion, the cost of illnesses caused by air pollution and medical care for victims of 2 million accidents a year. Other estimates range up to 12 per cent of GDP for America and 4.6 per cent for Europe.

During its lifetime an average car travels 200,000 miles, consuming over 3000 gallons of petrol and over 50 gallons of oil. It discharges more than 35 tons of carbon (*The Economist*, 22 June 1996).

[26] 777 million, if lorries and motorbikes are included. The projection is that the number of cars is likely to rise by 50 per cent by 2010 and double by 2030 (The *Economist*, op. cit.).

environmental, natural and financial resources that ought to be used to satisfy more fundamental social needs.

The motor car has been singled out only as *pars pro toto*. The same argument goes for many more items of conspicuous consumption.

The challenge for the South is to leapfrog to sustainable lifestyles avoiding the twin evils of waste and want, based on local cultures (but not on a fundamentalist respect of tradition) and on modern science and technology. Sustainable lifestyles need not be equated with monastic austerity.[27]

Richard Meier, a visionary architect who pioneered research on resource-saving cities, postulates a different civilization for Africa from those imagined in the parts of the world where the technologies evolved earlier.

The economy would have much less manufacturing and consumption of materials, but a greatly expanded supply of services. The wealth would reside in the human resources—the knowledge and health of the people and their organizations (Meier, R., 1996, p. 355).

His article has the merit of raising a fundamental question, even if it does not provide convincing solutions.

The main difficulty will be to persuade the South to give up the emulation of the consumption patterns of the North. As rightly observed by Gamani Corea (1989), a former Secretary-General of UNCTAD, there is a moral snag in the idea of one world with two lifestyles:

One life style in which the industrialized countries can keep to the habits that they have developed using up non-renewable resources, discharging toxic wastes and polluting both air and water? And another life style for the developing countries following a path of environmental soundness at the cost of lower levels of living, lower levels of productivity?

Corea's concludes that the

logic of the environmental debate points to the need for a revolution of lifestyles in the developed countries themselves so as to provide a

---

[27] As Romesh Thapar (1979, p. 7) has pointed out, these lifestyles should explore the confluences between two parallel streams of consciousness: 'One is concerned with the need to intensify all-round development and to assist the rapid movement into a twentieth century of life. The other represents a serious effort to preserve the best in inherited cultures and values, to resist unnecessary imitation and to locate the real essence of civilized life.'

model that can be pervasive, that can be valid throughout the world as a whole.

Leaving aside the question of one or many sustainable models, the North is under a compelling ethical imperative to question its lifestyles, consumerism and wasteful resource patterns for at least three reasons:

- their ecological, environmental and social unsustainability;
- the preemption on the part of the North of over three quarters of all the world's resources and of the limited ecological space;
- the negative demonstration effect on the South, referred to by Gamani Corea.

The example of the motor car shows that positive change can (and ought to) be brought through a combination of:

- investment in public transportation (intra- and inter-city rail);
- facilitating the use of bicycles;
- planning new human settlements in such a way as to minimize the need for transportation;
- last but not the least, improving the performance of the individual vehicle (electrical and hybrid cars, the light-weight 'hypercar' of Amory Lovins; green fuel, improving fuel economy by a factor of 2 or 3, etc.);
- replacement of travel by virtual mobility.

A more fundamental inquiry into alternative lifestyles would require analysing the different combinations of patterns of time-use and consumption.[28]

References

Albert, M. (1991), *Capitalisme contre capitalisme*, Le Seuil, Paris.
Arrow, K. et alii (1995), 'Economic Growth, Carrying Capacity, and the Environment', *Science*, 268, pp. 520–1; also *Ecological Economics*, 15, pp. 91–5.

[28] For a conceptual framework see Sachs, I., 'The Time-spaces of Development' in I. Sachs (1987).

Bariloche, Fundacion (1976), 'Catastrophe or New Society? A Latin-American World Model', IDRC, Ottawa.

Botkin, D. B. (1990), *Discordant Harmonies: A New Ecology for the 21st Century*, Oxford University Press, Oxford.

Brohman, J. (1996), *Popular Development—Rethinking the Theory and Practice of Development*, Blackwell, Oxford.

Corea, G. (1989), 'North must Change Life Styles', *South Letter*, October.

Costanza, R. and Patten, B. C. (1995), 'Defining and Predicting Sustainability', *Ecological Economics*, 15, pp. 193–6.

Daly, H. E. (1990), 'Toward Some Operational Principles of Sustainable Development', *Ecological Economics*, 2, pp. 1–6.

Diegues, A. C., Sant' Ana (1996), *O Mito Moderno da Natureza*, Hucitec, São Paulo.

Eder, K. (1996), *The Social Construction of Nature—A Sociology of Ecological Enlightenment*, Sage Publications, London.

Guimarães, R. P. (1994), 'El Desarrollo Sustenable: Propuesto Alternativa o Retorica Neoliberal?' *Revista EURE*, vol. XXI, n° 61, pp. 41–56.

Goulet, D. (1995), *Development Ethics: A Guide to Theory and Practice*, Apex Books, New York.

Heilbroner, R. (1993), *21st Century Capitalism*, W. W. Norton, New York.

Kapp, K. W. (1971), *The Social Costs of Private Enterprise*, Schocken Books, New York.

——— (1987), *Für eine ökosoziale ökonomie*, Entwürfe und Ideen, Ausgewählte Aufsätze.

Meier, R. (1996), 'A Hopeful Path for Development in Africa', *Futures*, vol. 28, n° 4, pp. 345–58.

'Monitoring Environmental Progress'—A Report on Work in Progress (1995), The World Bank, Washington, D. C.

Nerfin, M. (1986), 'Ni Prince ni Marchand: Citoyen—une introduction au tiers système', *IFDA Dossier* 56, novembre-décembre, pp. 3–29.

Polanyi, K. (1977), 'The Economistic Fallacy' in H. W. Pearon (ed.) *The Livelihood of Man*, Academic Press, New York.

Rapoport, A. (1974), *Conflict in Man-made Environment*, Penguin Books, Harmondsworth.

Report of the Commission on Global Governance: Our Global Neighbourhood (1995), Oxford University Press.

Rockefeller, S. C. (1996), 'The Emerging World Ethic and the Earth Charter Project', *Earth Ethics*, Spring–Summer, pp. 1–7.

Rostow, W. (1960), *From Trade-off to Self-sustained Growth*, 1960.

Sachs, I. (1974), 'Environment et styles de développement', *Anrales*, Economies, Sociétés, Civilisations, Paris, n° 3, mai-juin, pp. 55, 0.

———— (1979), *Studies in Political Economy of Development*, Pergamon Press, Oxford.

———— (1987), *Development and Planning*—Cambridge University Press, Cambridge, New York, New Rochelle; Paris, Ed. de la Maison des Sciences de l'Homme, p. 134.

———— (1993), *Transition Strategies towards the 21st Century*, Interest Publications, New Delhi.

———— (1994a), 'Population, Development and Employment', *International Social Science Journal*, no. 141, pp. 343–59, UNESCO–Blackwell Publishers, Oxford (UK).

———— (1994b), 'The Environmental Challenge', in Salomon, J. J., Sagasti, F. and Sachs-Jeantet, C. (eds), *The Uncertain Quest: Science, Technology and Development*, United Nations University Press, Tokyo.

———— (1995a), *Searching for New Development Strategies—The Challenges of the Social Summit*, MOST Policy Papers 1 prepared for the World Summit for Social Development, Copenhagen, 6–12 March, p. 48, UNESCO, Paris. Reprinted in *Economic and Political Weekly*, 8 July 1995.

———— (1995b), 'The Quantitative and Qualitative Measurement of Development—Its Implications and Limitations', in Measuring and Evaluating Development, *International Social Science Journal*, no. 143, March.

———— (1996), 'Overcoming Growth with Dedevelopment', (IDB Conference on Development Thinking and Practice, Washington, September).

Salomon, J J , Sagasti, F., Sachs-Jeantet, C. (eds) (1994), *The Uncertain Quest: Science, Technology and Development*, United Nations University Press, Tokyo.

Satterwhaite, D. (1996), 'For Better Living', *Down to Earth*, 31 July, pp. 31–5.

Sen, A. (1985), *Commodities and Capabilities*, North-Holland, Amsterdam.

———— (1987), *On Ethics and Economics*, Basil Blackwell, Oxford.

———— (1996), 'Development Thinking at the Beginning of the 21st Century', IDB Conference on Development Thinking and Practice, September, Washington.

Serageldin, I. and Steer, A. (eds) (1995), *Making Development Sustainable: From Concepts to Action*, The World Bank, Washington, D. C.

Serres, M. (1990), *Le contrat naturel*, François Bourin, Paris.

Thapar, R. (1979), 'Identity in Modernization', *Mainstream*, vol. XVII, no. 34, 21 April.

The Economist (1995), 'A Survey of Latin American Finance', prepared by Z. Minton-Beddoes, 9 December, p. 21.

—————— (1996),'Taming the Beast—A Survey on Living with the Car', 22 June, pp. 5–7.

UNDP (1995), *Human Development Report 1995*, New York.

UNEP (1980), 'Choosing the Options—Alternative Lifestyles and Development Patterns', Nairobi.

'What Now?' (1975), Dag Hammarskjöld Report on Development and International Cooperation, *Development Dialogue*, nr. 1/2.

Towards a Modern
Biomass-based Civilization[1]

'A new form of civilization based on the sustainable use of renewable resources is not only possible, but essential.' I fully share this opinion of the eminent Indian scholar M. S. Swaminathan.

In a sense, all the major civilizations of the past were biomass civilizations, insofar as they depended almost exclusively for their material life on biomass products: food-stuffs and animal feed (as it is still the case today), but also fuel, fibres for clothing, wood to build shelters and produce furniture, plants to heal. Even today millions of *ecosystem people*[2] -forest inhabitants and rural folk—still eke out their livelihoods from their immediate ecosystems often in a very ingenious way based on a deep knowledge of the working of the nature.

[1] This chapter draws from the keynote address at the International Workshop on Science and Technology for a Modern Biomass Civilization organized by COPPE/UFRJ and ENERGE in cooperation with the South–South Cooperation Programme on Environmentally Sound Socio-Economic Development in the Humid Tropics (UNESCO–MAB, UNU and TWAS) on the occasion of the Conference of the Third World Academy of Sciences, Rio de Janeiro, 8 September 1997.

[2] I borrow this expression from the excellent book by Madhav Gadgil and Ramachandra Guha (1995). The authors oppose the ecosystem people to 'omnivores' who tend to expropriate and expel the ecosystem people in order to satisfy their consumerist frenzy. See also Gadgil, M. and R. Guha (1993).

Our problem is not to go back to ancestral forms of living, but to transform the know-how of ecosystem people, collected through ethnosciences, into a starting point for the invention[3] of a *modern biomass civilization* situated at an entirely different point of the spiral of knowledge (and ascent of mankind). It is submitted that such a civilization will succeed in cancelling the enormous social debt accumulated over ages while at the same time, reducing the ecological debt.

For this, we ought to make the fullest use of frontier sciences, with special emphasis on biology and biotechnologies to explore the 'b cube' paradigm: *bio-bio-bio*, the first term standing for bio-diversity, the second for biomass and the third for biotechnologies.

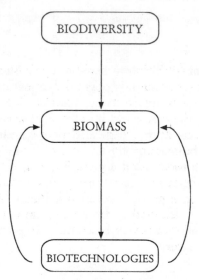

Fig. 3.1 The 'bio-cube paradigm'

A few words of explanation are in order here. The study of biodiversity should not be reduced to an inventory of species and genes for two reasons: firstly, because the concept of biodiversity also encompasses the ecosystems and the landscapes; secondly,

[3] 'Invention' is the right word, as we need new solutions instead of mimetic transposition of solutions evolved in other natural and socio-cultural environments. However, emphasis on indigenous development should not be mistaken for lack of interest in benefiting from other peoples' experience.

because biodiversity and cultural diversity are interwoven in the historical process of co-evolution.[4]

We need, therefore, a holistic and interdisciplinary approach in which social and natural scientists work together to evolve the wise ways of using nature while respecting its diversity.[5] Conservation and wise use of nature can and must go together. Here lies the challenge: how to conserve by choosing the right development strategies, rather than multiplying supposedly inviolable internal reserves? How to plan for multiple sustainable land and resource-use? How to design a diversified strategy of land occupation in which strict reserves and biosphere reserves have their place in setting of rules for the bulk of the territory put to productive use? The latter need not harm alongside the environment, nor destroy biodiversity so long as we understand that all our economic activities are ultimately embedded in a natural environment.

As already mentioned, biomass collected or produced on land and in water can be put to different uses. I borrow from Professor Jyoti Parikh the 'five–F' (Fig. 3.2) in which F stands for food, feed, fuel, fertilizer and industrialized feedstock.

The uses of biomass should be optimized by choosing the right combination of the five Fs within integrated food-energy systems adapted to different agro-climatic and socio-economic settings. This subject has been extensively discussed in Brazil, India and several other developing countries within the Food-energy Nexus Programme promoted by the United Nations University.[6] This programme emphasized the potential of man-made production systems imitating natural ecosystems. Our success in promoting sustainable development will to a great extent depend on our ability of designing such production systems and making them ever more productive by applying modern science.

Biotechnologies will play a major role in this endeavour at both extremes of the production chain by bringing about, on the one hand, increases in the productivity of biomass and, on the other

---

[4] Modern ecology increasingly resembles natural history. For an interesting presentation, see Botkin, D. B. (1990) and also C. and R. Larrère (1997).

[5] As C. and R. Larrère (*op. cit.*) point out, such a wise use ought to be informed by ecology and the techniques employed are regulated by ethical principles.

[6] See Sachs, I. (1990).

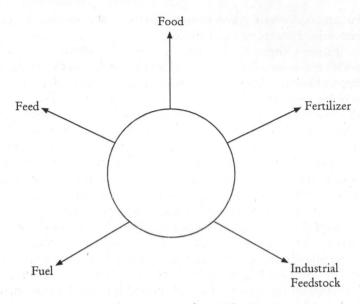

Fig. 3.2 Optimization of biomass uses (The five–F model)

hand, by opening up the range of products derived from it (see Fig. 3.1).

A major operational task, is how to make modern biotechnology available to small peasant farms, enabling them in this way to partake in the *second green revolution* (also called *doubly green revolution*).[7] Difficult as it may look, this is not an impossible endeavour although it implies a set of complementary policies (fair access to land, to knowledge, to credit and to markets, better rural education). Equally important for the prospect of a modern biomass civilization will be the efforts aimed at developing a *green chemistry* as a complement, if not a total substitute, of petrochemistry and at substituting bio-fuels for fossil energy.

For the tropical countries, this is a particularly challenging opportunity. Tropical climate, for a long time considered as a handicap, now appears as a lasting natural comparative advantage, insofar as biomass yields are higher there than in temperate zones. It is often said that natural resources have lost their importance in relation to human resources and knowledge. This is only partly

[7] See Griffon, M. and J. Weber (1995).

true. A good combination of abundant and cheap natural resources with skilled manpower and modern knowledge gives an unequalled comparative edge.

Of course, one has to take good care of fragile ecosystems and protect the population against tropical diseases. But we know how to overcome these constraints today, even though we still have a long way to go, before we succeed in these endeavours.

So, tropical countries in general, and Brazil in particular, have today a chance of leapfrogging[8] into an indigenous modern *three-win* biomass civilization simultaneously meeting the criteria of social pertinence, ecological prudence and economic viability, the three pillars of sustainable development (Fig. 3.3).

	IMPACTS		
	Economic	Social	Ecological
1. Savage growth	+	–	–
2. Socially benign growth	+	+	–
3. Environmentally sustainable growth	+	–	+
4. Development	+	+	+

Fig. 3.3: Patterns of growth[9]

Brazil was born, as Sergio Buarque de Holanda reminds us in the opening page of his celebrated essay,[10] out of an attempt to

[8] The importance of selective 'leapfrogging' in the process of development is being rightly emphasized by José Goldemberg (1996) who defines it as an early incorporation of state-of-the-art technologies by developing countries. Goldemberg then says that 'despite its attractiveness, 'leapfrogging' should not be regarded as a universal strategy, because sometimes the products or technologies needed are not available in developed countries, or are not well suited to the developing country needs' (p. 81). I would submit that the concept of 'leapfrogging' should be expanded so as to include original innovations obtained by developing countries ahead of the industrialized ones through concentration of research effort on selected particularly important topics.

[9] For a discussion of 'three win' solutions, see chapter 1 of Sachs (1995).

[10] See Buarque de Holanda, Sergio (1996, p. 31): 'The dominant feature in the origins of the Brazilian society, and the most relevant one by its consequences, are the attempts at implanting European culture on a large territory endowed with natural conditions which, without being adverse, were

transplant European culture on an extensive territory with conditions quite different from those familiar to the culture. Another Brazilian scholar, Gilberto Freyre, put forward the concept of *tropicalism*. One need not agree with him on what he had to say on the adaptation of Portuguese people in the tropical lands (*lusotropicalismo*) to recognize his pioneering vision of an original civilization of the tropics yet to be invented.[11] As a matter of fact, this is precisely the subject under discussion now.

One of the first Gilberto Freyre's writings on tropicalism dealt with the Amazon region. The efforts currently under way to produce an Agenda 21 for the Amazon region[12] refer explicitly to the context of biomass civilization. In order to set some priorities for science and technology required for a sustainable development strategy for the Amazon region, we may use as an entrypoint the division between the forested area and the area already deforested. Within the first category, we shall distinguish inhabited forests and forests with no human populations (virgin). In the second category, we shall consider separately the secondary forests (capoeiras) and all other areas. Fig. 3.4 illustrates some possible lines of action for a wise use of nature in the Amazon region.

A stands for indigenous reserves, B for extractive and biosphere reserves and C for cities and towns.

1 stands for multi-level family agrosilviculture, adapted to rain tropical ecosystems and closely following the architecture of the forest; 2 stands for enriched forests; 3 stands for plantations; 4 stands for harvesting of non-wood forest products and selective cutting of timber (the dotted line denotes the unwillingness of timber companies to exploit secondary forests, their strategy consisting mainly of first cuttings in the primeval forests); and 5 stands for other environmentally benign productions (with special reference to the domestication of local animal and vegetable species).

---

alien to its millenary tradition....For sure, all the fruits of our work, or of our laziness, seem to partake of an evolutionary system belonging to another climate and another landscape.'

[11] For an interesting analysis of Gilberto Freyre's tropicalism, see the essay by Benchimol, S. in Pavan, C. (ed.) vol. 2, (1996a), pp. 345-9. For a general evaluation of Gilberto Freyre's work, see Ribeiro, Darcy (1997).

[12] *Agenda 21 for Amazonia* (1997).

Forests		Deforested Areas	
Virgin	Inhabited	Secondary Forests	Other
	A B		C
	①		
	②		
	③		
	④		
	⑤		

Fig. 3.4 Possible lines of action for a wise use of nature in the Amazon region

With these objectives in view, we may now turn to the priorities for research. The following ten suggestions are by no means exhaustive. Their purpose is only illustrative.

1. We certainly need a better understanding of the working of the diverse ecosystems in the Amazon region.[13] The Large Biosphere Atmosphere initiative appears as an important step in this direction.[14]

2. Side by side, with research based on macro data, one has to proceed with the setting of local data banks on biodiversity. Some pioneering work in India shows the possibility of achieving this goal while keeping the control over these banks in local hands.

---

[13] The Amazon region encompasses many ecosystems. Aziz N. Ab'Saber is right to insist on the need to consider the emerging problems of each of the 27 sub-regions. See his contributions in Sachs, I. and M. Clüsener-Godt (eds) (1995), pp. 287–303 and to Pavan, C. (ed.) (1996b), vol. 3, pp. 56–105.

[14] 'The Large Scale Biosphere-Atmosphere Experiment in Amazonia (LBA)—Concise Experimental Plan', INPE, Cachoeira Paulista (SP), April 1996.

3. For reasons already explained, the study of biological and cultural diversity ought to be conducted as a joint endeavour involving teams of natural and social scientists; a greatly increased effort in this direction is called for.

4. The sustainable use of biodiversity requires at the same time the capacity to conduct advanced research in the field of molecular ecology along the lines suggested by the programme PROBEM/ Amazonia recently proposed by the Secretariat for the Coordination of Amazonian Affairs (Ministry of Environment) and the Butantan Institute (University of São Paulo).

5. The study of integrated production systems adapted to local conditions must proceed at different scales of production from the family farm to fairly large commercial systems; both have their place in a sustainable development strategy.

6. An important subject for research is the design of equipment for harvesting, transportation and processing of forest products, including unconventional carries (zeppelins) and mobile processing units (on rivers).

7. Diverse local energy production systems (biomass-based, small-scale hydro, wind-powered and solar) ought to be designed and tested.

8. A neglected yet important area of research is the modernization of the techniques employed by the subsistence household subsector; improving the working of this subsector has a direct impact on the livelihood of the concerned populations releasing furthermore some labour power for market-oriented activities.

9. Modernization of existing production systems can take the form of their complexification by successively adding new production modules; the already mentioned possibility of domesticating local species, adding pisciculture to family farms, etc., come into the picture here.

10. Designing of delivery systems for social services (education, health) adapted to the specific conditions of rural Amazonia with its dispersed populations along the rivers looms large as a priority of research, insofar as greater access to such services is crucial for a more efficient functioning of the production systems and for improving the living conditions; the same goes for the communication both as an access to some cultural amenities and to the much needed information on market conditions, etc.

The above list presents a tall but not an impossible order. The important thing to note is that it cuts across many fields of knowledge. Inventing a modern biomass civilization should not be left to laboratory people alone, although their contribution will be by all means decisive. Fortunately, we are not starting from scratch. In Brazil, India and several other countries, considerable work on the subject has been already accomplished and a lot more is in the offing. The Rio de Janeiro Workshop has been designed to review the Brazilian research on biomass utilization and confront it with the experiences of India[15] as well as some other countries. The choice of the date and of the venue is symbolic. The meeting is being held simultaneously with the Conference of the Third World Academy of Sciences and its conclusions will be presented to that *egregious* body in the hope that it will actively promote South–South cooperation around the theme of modern biomass civilization.

Let me end by restating my firm belief that progress along this road can assist the developing countries in inventing their endogenous development patterns, which are more equitable and, at the same time, respectful of nature. Harnessing of the biomass potential of the tropics offers Third World scientists an opportunity to leapfrog ahead of the industrialized countries. And by making a wise use of nature, tropical countries will be contributing to the wise global management of the biosphere. As a recent report put it, Brazil and other tropical countries have all the conditions to become *exporters of sustainability* (IPEA, 1997, pp. 156–8) thus transforming the environmental challenge into an opportunity.

References

'*Agenda 21 for Amazônia—Basis for Discussion* (1997), Ministry of the Environment, Water Resources and the Legal Amazonia, Secretariat for the Coordination of Amazonian Affairs, Brasilia, March 1997.
Benchimol, S. (1996), 'Borealismo Ecologico e Tropicalismo Ambiental', in Pavan, C. (ed.), *Uma Estratégia Latino-Americana para a Amazônia*, vol. 2, MMA:Memorial/Ed. UNESP, São Paulo, pp. 345–9.

[15] In addition to the papers prepared for this workshop by Professors Shukla and Vinicius Nobre Lages, the following two books deserve special attention: Ravindranath, N. H. and D. O. Hall (1995) and Venkata Ramana, P. and S. N. Srinivas (eds) (1997).

Botkin, D. B. (1990), *Discordant Harmonies: A New Ecology for the 21st Century,* Oxford University Press, Oxford.

Buarque de Holanda, S. (1996), *Raizes do Brasil,* Companhia Nacional de Letras, São Paulo, p. 31.

Gadgil, M. and Guha, R. (1993), *This Fissured Land: An Ecological History of India,* Oxford University Press, Delhi.

——— (1995), *Ecology and Equity: The Use and Abuse of Nature in Contemporary India,* Penguin Books, New Delhi.

Goldemberg, J. (1996), *Energy, Environment and Development,* Earthscan, London.

Griffon, M. and Weber, J. (1995), *La révolution doublement verte: économie et institutions.* Séminaire URPA, Futuroscope de Poitiers, p. 6.

IPEA (1997), 'O Brasil na Virada do Milêino—Trajetoria do crescimento e desafios do desenvolvimento', *Brasilia,* Julho, pp. 156-8.

Larrère, C. and R. (1997), *Du bon usage de la nature—Pour une philosophie de l'environnement,* Aubier, Paris.

Pavan, C. (ed.) (1996a), *Uma Estratégia Latino-Americana para a Amazônia,* vol. 2, MMA/Memorial/Ed. UNESP, São Paulo, pp. 345-9.

——— (1996b), *Uma Estratégia Latino-Americana para a Amazônia,* vol. 3, MMA/Memorial/Ed. UNESP, São Paulo, pp. 56-105.

Ravindra, N. H. and Hall, D. O. (1995), *Biomass, Energy and Environment—A Developing Country Perspective from India,* Oxford University Press, Oxford-New York-Tokyo.

Ribeiro, D. (1997), *Gentidades,* L&PM, Porto Alegre, pp. 7-89.

Sachs, I. (1990) (in collaboration with D. Silk), *Food and Energy: Strategies for Sustainable Development,* United Nations University Press, p. 83, Tokyo.

——— (1995), *Searching for New Development Strategies: The Challenges of the Social Summit,* MOST Policy Papers 1 prepared for the World Summit for Social Development, Copenhagen, 6-12 March, p. 48, UNESCO, Paris.

Sachs, I. and Clüsener-Godt, M. (eds) (1995), *Brazilian Perspectives on Sustainable Development of the Amazon Region,* UNESCO, Parthenon, Paris-Carnforth-New York, pp. 287-303.

Venkata Ramana, P. and Srinivas, S. N. (eds) (1997), *Biomass Energy Systems.* Proceedings of the International Conference, 26-7 February 1996, New Delhi, Tata Energy Research Institute.

4

Developing in a Liberalized and Globalizing World Economy: An Impossible Challenge?

What should be the end of man and how should he choose his means?
Economic rationalism, in the strict sense, has no answer to these questions,
for they imply motivations and valuations of a moral and practical order
that go beyond the irresistible, but otherwise empty, exhortation to be
'economical'.

KARL POLYANYI, 'The Economistic Fallacy'

Mais où trouver le médecin prudent qui tracera les lois de l'hygiène
monétaire, et fournira les moyens d'éviter les accidents?

HONORÉ DE BALZAC, Code des gens honnêtes
ou l'art de ne pas être dupe des fripons,

Between Rhetoric and Reality: A Semantic Prologue

Words matter, mostly when they are polysemic. Communication becomes exceedingly difficult, or even impossible, when people use the same word to denote different things without explicating its actual meaning. Other semantic traps to beware of, are the 'diplomacy by terminology' exposed by Gunnar Myrdal[1] and mistaking *mantra* chanting for problem solving.

---

[1] Within a short span of time 'backward' countries became successively known as 'underdeveloped', 'less developed' and, finally, 'developing', while their actual condition did not change much.

The catch word nowadays is 'globalization'. Its popularity is partly due to the fact that it refers to four partly overlapping phenomena.

Thus, globalization denotes the emergency (more exactly the growing awareness) of *global problems* affecting all the passengers of the Spaceship Earth irrespective of whether they travel first or third class, (although the implications for each category are different): the climatic change caused by the emission of green-house gases, pandemics such as AIDS,[2] drug addiction, terrorism and, last but not the least, social exclusion as a worldwide phenomenon.

History has played a cruel joke on us. Rapid economic growth, through its 'trickle-down effects', was supposed to ensure prosperity to all. In post-colonial, peripheral countries the expansion of the modern sector would gradually absorb, it was thought, the entire workforce of the traditional sector bringing it in this way to extinction. Instead, the dualization processes took hold of the advanced industrial countries and the spectre of 'social apartheid' menaces rich and poor countries alike.

But globalization also means *global thinking*, looking at the world as a whole. Globalism has always permeated imperialistic doctrines and shaped the policies of big powers, of which only one is left on the scene at present, after the demise of the Soviet Union and the dislocation of the bipolar international system. Within one single tragic century two world wars, and many other of a more restricted nature, resulted from the clash of conflicting global endeavours (see Hobsbawm, E., 1994).

Universalism, the often betrayed heritage of the European Enlightenment,[3] is poles apart from the globalism as defined above. It affirms the existence of a set of perennial values shared by all human beings, enshrined in the Charter of the United Nations and the compact of human rights. Those values should inform all the actions taken by governments and international

---

[2] The microbian unification of the world preceded the creation of a world economy.

[3] For an interesting analysis of how the heritage of the *Lumières* is being perverted in the North, see Guillebaud, J. C. (1995). The author observes that the critics from the South are less sanguine about the universalist pretense of our values, than about our infidelity to the *Lumières*. 'It is not the strength of our principles that is questioned, but their betrayal' (p. 35).

organizations with a view at promoting the fundamental objectives of peace and development. Taken to its logical extreme, universalism postulates the establishment of a world government or at least of a functional confederation of international organizations, decentralized at the operational level and centralized at the policy-making level, the ultimate aim being 'decentralized planetary sovereignty' (J. Tinbergen et al. coordinators, 1976, p. 84).

Finally, in a more restrictive sense, globalization is used to describe 'a process whereby producers and investors increasingly share as if the world economy consisted of a single market and production area with regional subsectors, rather than of a set of national economies linked by trade and investment flows' (UNCTAD, 1996, p. 6).

The most extreme globalizers[4] pretend that this process has advanced to the point of becoming irreversible and so overwhelming that it deprives the Nation-States of effective power of regulation over their economics. The only two forces that matter are the global markets and the transnational companies. Neither can be subject to effective public governance. However, this view is challenged in a well-argued book by Hirst and Thompson (1996).

For them, globalization is to a large extent a myth.[5] The present highly globalized economy is not unprecedented.[6] Genuinely

[4] Such as e.g. Ohmae, Kenichi (1996) or Naisbitt, John (1995).

[5] See also Bairoch, P. (1996), Streeten, P. (1996), Ferrer, A. (1996a) and Guaino, M. (1996). Rather than condemning Nation-States, globalization forces them to compete. Planning remains an important tool of coherence, cohesion and harmonization. Among American economists, P. Krugman (1994) has repeatedly denounced the danger of paying too much importance to the globalization problems to the detriment of domestic development. For a more fundamental treatment of the globalization processes and theories, see Ferrer, A. (1996b) and Ianni, O (1995). In France, the list of books dealing with globalization grows at a very impressive rate. For a thorough and balanced analysis of the implications of globalization for France, see Cohen, E. (1996) and Brender, A. (1996).

[6] Deepak Nayyar (1995) traces an illuminating parallel between the globalization processes of the last quarter of the twentieth century and the 1870–1914 period. According to the South Centre (1996a), the extent of trade openness among industrial countries was then fairly similar to that of today. For 16 of the most advanced countries the share of exports in GDP was 18.2 per cent in 1990 and 21.2 per cent in 1913. During the present era, the share of world exports in world GDP has increased from less than 6 per cent in 1950

transnational companies are relatively few. Most companies which trade multinationally are nationally based, and maintain a close relationship with their respective governments. Capital mobility is not producing a massive shift of investment and employment from the advanced to the developing countries. Far from being genuinely 'global', the world economy is concentrated in the Triad (North America, Europe, Japan). The major advanced nations continue to be dominant. About 80 per cent of world trade is conducted between the OECD countries. The group of five main economies accounts for 70 per cent of foreign direct investment, whose importance is often overstated. Indeed, the most significant recent development is the formation of regional economic blocs such as the European union, NAFTA and, lately on, Mercosur. The globalization myth serves a double purpose:

– to accredit the notion that an international order[7] has at last emerged rendering obsolete the claims advanced in the seventies by the Non-Aligned Movement and the Group of 77, and

– to undermine the efforts of the Nation-States to improve their ability to regulate their economies and design development strategies.

Hirst and Thompson believe that the international economy can still be controlled and national development strategies has not yet lost their relevance. One of the main contentions of their book is that 'Nation-States have a significant role to play in economic governance at the level of both national and international processes' (p. 170).

Yet, the condition to it is to address the right questions. The UNCTAD Report, quoted above, states that 'globalization is the

---

to 12 per cent in 1973 and 16 per cent in 1992. The corresponding figures for industrial countries are 12 per cent in 1973 and 17 per cent in 1992. The stock of direct foreign investment in the world as a proportion of world output was broadly the same in 1992 (8.4 per cent) as it was in 1913 (9.0 per cent).

[7] Speaking at the India International Centre in January 1996, the Brazilian President, Fernando Henrique Cardoso, stated: 'whether we wish it or not, globalization is a new international order. We must accept this fact with a sense of realism. Otherwise our actions will lack effective impact. This is not tantamount to political inertia, but an entirely new perspective on forms of action on the international scene' (p. 33).

product of liberalization' (p. 7). Significantly, its first chapter bears the following title: 'Trade and Development in a Liberalized and Globalizing World Economy'. Globalization is a process fueled by liberalization perceived as a *fait accompli*.[8]

What would be left for regulation by Nation-States in an economy fully liberalized, internally and externally? Fortunately, up to now no purely *laissez-faire* economy has ever existed, in which resources are allocated entirely by the totally unrestricted market under conditions of unlimited competition. As Eric Hobsbawm (1994, pp. 563–5) has observed, such a counter-utopia to the collapsed real socialism is also demonstrably bankrupt. All the 'miracles' of the twentieth century were accomplished not through the *laissez-faire* but against it. A more serious question than the breakdown of two polar extremes is the disorientation of the middle-path programmes and policies, that combine pragmatically public and private, market and planning, state and business.

Let us move now to *development*. Faced with the global problem of poverty, unemployment and social exclusion, the Copenhagen Declaration reaffirmed the commitment of the United Nations to the concept of sustainable development in which the social, economic and environmental dimensions are closely interwoven (Nations, Unies, 1995, p. 4). Development, as understood today, is a comprehensive concept distinct from economic growth, still viewed as a necessary, but by no means a sufficient condition, encompassing ethical, political, social, ecological, economic, cultural and territorial dimensions, all of them systemically interrelated and forming a 'whole'. The evolutionary nature of development calls, furthermore, for considering its sustainability (perennity) in order to meet the ethical postulate of diachronic solidarity with the future generations, symmetrical to the postulate of synchronic solidarity with the present generation, which in turn accounts for the preeminence of social considerations in the setting of developmental objectives (Sachs, I., 1993).

Although brought into the debate by environmental concerns, sustainability has as many facets as development itself. It is suggested that, given the multiplicity and, sometimes, redundancy of adjectives successively added to development in the course of

[8] For a masterly analysis of the consequences of liberalization on a developing country (in this case India) see Badhuri, A. and D. Nayyar (1996).

a half-century long debate—the latest being human[9]—a better denomination might be *whole development.*[10] Whole stands as a shorthand for all the attributes of development, indicating at the same time that all the pertinent dimensions are contemplated in their interrelatedness, so that the conceptual model is *complete* and *holistic.*

The Social Summit: An Assessment *en clair-obscur*

The Copenhagen Declaration should be read in conjunction with the Rio Declaration adopted at the 1992 Earth Summit. Both are built around the concept of human-centred sustainable development and consider eradication of poverty as a condition *sine qua non* of such development.

Both proclaim the *right to development.* Albeit the Copenhagen Declaration, incorporating the results of the 1993 UN Conference on Human Rights, does it in a more explicit and solemn manner, as an integral part of fundamental human rights.[11] One way of reconceptualizing development might consist in looking at it in terms of *universalizing the effective appropriation of all human rights*—civil, political, but also social, economic and cultural. Such an approach seems to offer both theoretical and operational advantages: it allows for escaping from narrow 'economicism' and, at the same time, provides a framework for the concrete evaluation of the progress (or regress) achieved on the tormented path from maldevelopment to development.[12]

[9] The UNDP publishes annual reports on Human Development and also proposed a synthetic (and, as far as I am concerned, controversial) index of human development (see Sachs, I., 1995b). At any rate, a more appropriate word in English would be 'humane'.

[10] For F. Perroux development concerns '*tout* l'homme et *tous* les hommes'.

[11] The very notion of 'right to development' has been fiercely resisted by the Republican administration in the USA. The Copenhagen Declaration and Action Plan mention it repeatedly. One would have expected, however, a more elaborated substantive statement on this fundamental subject whose codification is overdue.

[12] However, even the right to be decently fed has been contested on conceptual grounds by the American delegation at the recent Food Security Summit in Rome. Clearly, the American establishment would not like to see the 'rights to development' approach applied to the United States given the downward spiral of social indicators and a severely declining quality of life

In this context, the objective of full employment, unambiguously reaffirmed in Copenhagen, appears as central to the implementation of economic and social rights. The more so that unemployment and severe underemployment affect 30 per cent of the world work force and that realistic projections do not warrant any optimism unless employment-oriented development strategies replace the growth-oriented ones.

Under the circumstances two attitudes were possible:

– the one adopted, to the credit of the Copenhagen Summit, of reaffirming the centrality of full employment; or,

– proclaiming the obsolescence of the very notion of work, superseded by that, somewhat ambiguous, of activity and indulging into one more exhortation about the need for a fundamental shift in the civilizational paradigm. While fully recognizing the importance of the latter debate for the shaping of long-term solutions (see Appendix 1), generation of employment and self-employment *hic et nunc* should be considered as the cornerstone of meaningful development strategies. It should be used as an entry point into their formulation, rather than being treated as a mere outcome of decisions related to growth of output and of productivity of labour subordinated to the relentless pursuit of competitiveness by means of an

---

in that country (see Miringoff, M. L. et al., 1996). Let it be also said that, contrary to a widely publicized view, properly counted the unemployment rate in the United States is not better than Europe's. According to Lester Thurow (1996b, p. 56), 'If we combine the 7.5 to 8 million officially unemployed workers, the 5 to 6 million people who are not working but who do not meet any of the tests for being active in the workforce and are therefore not considered unemployed, and the 4.5 million part-time workers who could like full-time work, there are 17 to 18.5 million Americans looking for more work. This brings the real unemployment rate to almost 14 per cent. Slow growth has also generated an enormous contingent workforce of underemployed people. There are 8.1 million American workers in temporary jobs, 2 million who work "on call", and 8.3 million self-employed "independent contractors" (many of whom are downsized professionals who have very few clients but call themselves self-employed consultants because they are too proud to admit that they are unemployed). Most of these more than 18 million people are also looking for more work and better jobs. Together these contingent workers account for another 14 per cent of the workforce'.

ever-accelerating 'creative destruction.[13] It is submitted that: the prospect for the generation of employment and self–employment through appropriate public policies is less grim than usually acknowledged (see Sachs, 1994b and Appendix 2).

However, such policies require from the Nation-States a capacity for intervention that the liberalization processes have undermined, if not entirely destroyed.

Unfortunately, both the Rio and Copenhagen declarations failed to raise this issue, indulging in ambiguous statements about the opening of economies and globalization.

Although the incompatibility of sustainable development with the unrestricted work of market forces has been repeatedly pointed out in the preparatory work for the Earth Summit,[14] the Rio Declaration did not address this issue explicitly, limiting itself to ask the States to 'reduce and eliminate unsustainable patterns of production and consumption'. It further asked the States, in most general terms, 'to promote a supportive and open international economic system that would lead to economic growth and sustainable development in all countries', a way of begging the question.

The Copenhagen Declaration takes a stance in favour of dynamic, open and free markets, while recognizing the need to intervene in these markets 'to the necessary extent' (whatever it means), in order to prevent or correct their failures. It mentions liberalization several times as a *solution*, never as part of the *problem*, as it should be (Guimarãe, R. P., 1996). In particular, the signatories of the Declaration commit themselves to accelerate the liberalization of trade and investment so as to favour sustainable economic growth and employment generation. The Declaration

---

[13] At what point does 'creative destruction' become counter-productive? When Schumpeter coined this concept he had in mind much lower rates of rotation of fixed capital. Computers and other equipment become *morally obsolete* (Marx) at such a speed that an ever-increasing volume of investment goes into premature reposition, to the detriment of employment-augmenting investment. The problem is compounded by the already mentioned diversion of financial resources from productive investment to speculation.

[14] See in particular the contributions of two Nobel Prize winners, T. Haavelmo and J. Tinbergen in the volume edited by Goodland, Daly, El Serafy and Von Droste (1991). See also Sachs (1993).

takes as granted that increase of incomes, growth of employment and expansion of trade mutually reinforce each other. It proposes to monitor in the developing countries the impact of the trade liberalization on the improved satisfaction of the basic needs of the population, apparently assuming that this impact can only be positive.

The Programme of Action states that globalization and the rapid technical progress reinforce labour mobility creating new possibilities of employment *while making the future uncertain.* This is a very peculiar way of addressing the issue of jobless growth and of the phenomenon of de-industrialization occuring provoked in several Third World and post–socialist countries as a consequence of unselective opening of their economies.

Liberalization and globalization are neither an absolute evil nor the magic shortcut to the kingdom of prosperity and happiness. They produce winners and loosers within countries and between countries, a *global North* and a *global South,* whose boundaries cut across all nations. The gap between them widens. The rich and the poor people are living in increasingly separated worlds.[15] This trend will not be reverted by merely continuing the liberalization and globalization processes in their present form. They must be brought under closer control, nationally and internationally, and submitted to tighter rules of the game. Copenhagen has sinned by omission. It did not sufficiently analyse the indepth causes of the evil. In consequence, it got entangled with modern Sisyphus' works: reactive social policies bringing relief to the victimized populations dealing with unemployed and excluded, rather than with unemployment and exclusion.[16]

But, to conclude on a more cheerful note, the Social Summit held at Copenhagen created a political momentum, which will

[15] 'An emerging global elite, mostly urban-based and interconnected in a variety of ways, is amassing great wealth and power, while more than half of the humanity is left out.' J. Speth, UNDP administrator presenting the *1996 Human Development Report,* reported in *International Herald Tribune,* 16 July 1996. More than 3 billion people live on an income of less than 2 dollars per day.

[16] Cf. Philippe Séguin (1996, p. 26): 'Terrible contresens: on s'échine à traiter les chômeurs, alors qu'il faudrait traiter le chômage'. Remedial social policies are certainly necessary, given the growing numbers of people who must be assisted. But they do not attack the problem at its roots.

hopefully bring into debate the right questions. It is time to open the hidden agenda.

Overhauling National Governance

According to Broad and Cavanagh (1995), global markets integrate about one-third of humanity, most of those in the rich countries plus the elite of poor countries. Country-wise, the North–South gap is narrowing for about a dozen countries but continues to widen for well over 100 others. 'Without a major shift in policy, the world of the twenty-first century will be one of economic apartheid' (p. 24).

Which will be the fortunate few developing countries to benefit from the integration with the world economy through globalization? For Deepak Nayyar (op. cit., p. 26) the only countries that stand a chance are those which have laid the requisite foundations for industrialization and development. For this, strategic forms of State intervention are essential, along with the creation of institutions capable of regulating, governing and facilitating the functioning of markets.[17] In their absence, globalization will reproduce, once more, *uneven development*. Though globalization has reduced the autonomy of the Nation-State, some degrees of freedom remain and must be used to create economic space for the pursuit of national interests and development objectives.

The same is true of Nation-States in industrial countries. The disaffected workers there, marginalized by the global economy, need the Nation-State 'as a buffer from the world economy' notes E. B. Kapstein (1996, p. 16) complaining about the demise of governments For him 'the fate of the global economy ultimately rests on domestic policies in its constituent States'.

In his report on globalization and liberalization, the Secretary-General of UNCTAD insists on the role of the State in providing an appropriate enabling environment for private enterprise, in dealing with environmental externalities and in addressing issues of poverty and income distribution. This 'mild' version of interventionism is predicated on reliance on market forces as the primary means for the allocation of resources and the organization

---

[17] The neoliberal theology misses a fundamental point made by K. Polanyi: markets are social constructs (see Bagnasco, A., 1988).

of economic activity. It falls within the range of European models of governance of social democrat inspiration.[18]

It is my belief that to meet the present challenges a stronger version is called for, questioning one of the basic tenets of the social democrat paradigm: the possibility of ensuring equity through *redistribution of income* without interfering in the problems of *production* and *consumption*.

In the real world, which does not resemble the ideal model of perfect competition and democratic transparency, the so-called market forces (and the power groups behind them) tend to promote a perverse pattern of *growth through inequality* or even *growth with dedevelopment* (Sachs, 1996). At some point this trend must be arrested because of its disruptive social effects and the excessive cost of policies aimed merely at their 'alleviation' (not a very glorious objective).[19] What matters really is the *primary distribution of income* inherent to the production paradigm, the corresponding employment structure and the *access to assets* and resources.

As a matter of fact, *equality of chances*, another tenet of the social democrat paradigm, can only be achieved by democratizing the access to *collective equipments* (i.e. assets) such as housing, transportation, urban environment, credit, side by side with education and health (Fitoussi, J. P. et Rosanvallon, P., 1996, pp. 210 and 228). In this context, one realizes the importance of a concept central to the French model: *public services* neither entirely public nor entirely private, 'a negotiated third way based on the redefinition of the relationships public/private' (Rachline, F., 1996, p. 28).

At the same time, a caveat should be entered with respect to the overestimation of the impact of education as a lever of employment. Training per se will not generate jobs. Whom to train? For what jobs? Created by whom? Say's law and supply economics will not work in the information age, no more than up to now.[20]

---

[18] For a recent analysis of competing models of capitalism, continuing the work of A. Schonfield and M. Albert, see Crouch and Streeck, 1996.

[19] My stance is diametrically opposed to that of the OECD experts, who consider that the struggle against unemployment requires the widening of inqualities. See on this point, Halimi, S., 1996.

[20] See e.g. Phelps, E. S. (1996) and Ph. Séguin (op. cit.) In the already quoted article E.B. Kapstein writes: 'It is odd that training has become the mom and apple pie of economists and public officials across the political spectrum when

Another powerful reason to modify the production *and* the consumption patterns—an even more daring task given the present balance of power—stems from environmental considerations. Consumerism, as we practise it in the industrial countries with its profligate use of fossil energy is not sustainable in the long run, and its reproduction in the South for the benefit of its elites is not possible without maintaining a severe *social apartheid* there.

The need to change consumption patterns and lifestyles of the rich, in order to make possible the economic and social advance for the poor, has been proclaimed in several international conferences since Stockholm, including the Copenhagen Summit. Both the Declaration and the Action programme see the main cause of environmental degradation in the unsustainable patterns of consumption and production, mainly in industrial countries. But, to my knowledge, little has been done up to now beyond rhetorical recognition of the problem and moral exhortation *et pour cause*. In *market societies* States hesitate for doctrinal reasons (the consumer sovereignty) to use the means of regulation available to them (fiscal systems, public investment, etc.). As for the former centrally planned economies, they completely misused their capacity to influence consumption patterns and to adequately face the environmental challenge.

Unless one considers that the collapse of command economies is a proof *a contrario* of the excellence of the liberal capitalist model (which would be a folly), the challenge before us is to rethink in its entirety the *modalities of regulation of mixed economies*, rather than to choose from the range of existing models of capitalism. Practically all the post-communist countries, with the possible exception of China, took the imitative and not the innovative way, thus missing a historic opportunity. However, the future must be *invented*. Heilbroner and Milberg (1995) are right when they point to a crisis of vision in modern economic thought.

This is a much too ambitious task to be attempted here.[21] I shall limit myself to enunciate questions that could serve as entry-points into this matter:

---

it could at best provide only a partial answer to the problems of dislocated workers....' (op. cit. pp. 27–8).

[21] In November 1989, in the wake of the fall of the Berlin wall, I proposed a comparative project on 'mixed economies' summarized in Appendix 3.

- what are the different development alternatives available to a State?
- how to articulate the internal development with a sovereign insertion in the world economy?[22]
- is national planning still relevant, and, in the affirmative, under what form?[23]
- what content should be given to democracy beyond mere compliance with the rules of the game of representative democracy?
- how to achieve new forms of partnership among the State, the civil society and the business world so as to enhance and bring out the full potential of local initiatives and citizen actions?
- in the absence of an equitable and efficient international order, what kind of national safeguards are required to protect the economy from disruptive and deleterious effects of decisions taken by external economic and financial agents?[24]

This bring us to the next point.

Globalization and International Governance

Equity in international economy relations requires rules of the game biased in favour of the weaker partner (G. Myrdal). UNCTAD was formed on this principle. Formal equality between partners of unequal strength creates, on the contrary, highly asymmetrical

---

[22] It is necessary to transcend the dichotomy between the inward-looking and outward-looking growth searching for a 'development from within' (Sunkel, O., 1993).

[23] Personally, I believe that the collapse of central planning should not be interpreted as the end of planning as such. All big corporations do strategic planning. Why should the Nation-State abstain? The French experience suggests that consultation among all the protagonists of the development process may lead to interesting results, mostly when the interested parties establish between themselves *contractual* linkages. The Nordic concept of *negotiated economy* points to the same direction.

[24] It is paradox of history that, forgetful of their historical experience, under the pressure of globalizers Nation-States consent to dismantle their defences at the interface with the world economy, i.e. at the point where they are most vulnerable.

relations of domination of the weaker by the stronger. Yet, this is the direction in which the international system is moving after the defeat of the proposals for the NIEO, put forward by the developing countries in the seventies.

In its present form, the system is both inefficient and unequitable, unable to 'civilize' the globalization processes and effectively assist the development efforts. Reshaping the international order is urgently called for, a complex, exceedingly difficult and time-consuming endeavour. Meanwhile, reliance on internal safeguards remains the main option.

Curbing the tyranny of international financial markets is the first priority. The IMF, the IBS (Basel), the World Bank and the central banks are unable to bring them under control. Governments, which have liberalized the financial markets, find it very difficult to resist the wanderings of the volatile capital and to the outbursts of speculation.[25] The phenomenal growth of private financial transactions, completely delinked from the real economy, diverts resources from productive investment and has pushed up the real rates of interest to unprecedented levels; infrastructural investment is the first casualty.

The vulnerability of the system is so evident, that some farseeing financial operators demand the overhauling of the Bretton Woods institutions and setting up tighter rules. For George Soros (1996), the present day economy rests on a very fragile basis. Markets are imperfect and can be brought to collapse in the absence of strong mechanisms ordering the globalized economy. 'An open society that is not ruled by laws is unviable—be it a country or a planet. At present the international finance does not obey any law. When an activity escapes the realm of law, it is force that prevails' (p. 10).

Already twenty years ago, James Tobin suggested a tax on foreign-exchange transactions,[26] whose daily turnover has grown now to around 1.2 trillion of dollars.[27] Such a tax would curb the

---

[25] The success story of South Korea and Taiwan contrasted with the experience of Latin America (see, Singh, A., 1996) and then the South Korean crisis due to excessive financial liberalization are very instructive indeed. See on this, Chapter 6 below.

[26] See Haq et al. (1996) for an up-to-date analysis of this proposal and the controversies around it.

[27] According to *The Economist* (13 July 1996) the daily turnover is roughly the same as the total currency reserves of the world's central banks.

short-run speculation. Besides, it would generate huge amounts of resources. A tax of one per thousand (0.1 per cent)—a dime on a dime on a dime—would yield about 150 billion dollars, enough to ensure on a worldwide scale the implementation of Agenda 21 and to provide at last the United Nations with an automatic source of financing.[28]

The Copenhagen Summit practically ignored the Tobin proposal, limiting itself to an appeal for an additional foreign assistance. Meanwhile, the ratio of ODA to industrial countries' GNP has shrunk to a historical low. Under the pressure of the Republican majority in the Congress, the United States are disengaging themselves from multilateral assistance.

Without a worthwhile international monetary system, fairly stable exchange rates and aligned currencies, a trading system cannot operate in an orderly manner. This is a serious handicap for the system that is being built around the WTO, but by no means its only weakness. For Muchkund Dubey (1996), a former Indian ambassador to the United Nations and to GATT, 'the international trading system that has emerged from the Uruguay Round is a combination of highly qualified and only partially liberal multilateralism, discriminatory regionalism and arbitrary unilateralism' (p. 130). The regime of Intellectual Property Rights is a move away from liberalism and competition. Trade in agriculture will still remain largely shackled. No international regime has been contemplated to curb restrictive business practices of the TNCs. The regional integration schemes will tend to marginalize the countries staying outside these arrangements. No wonder that he titled his book, *An Unequal Treaty*.

The logical consequence he draws from this analysis for India is a plea to 'resume the path of self-reliant growth without isolating ourselves from the rest of the world' (p. 134). Integration with the global economy should be selective and development of technological capability reinforced. Financial liberalization should come last in the sequence of economic reforms. 'All attempts to use the financial powers of the IMF and World Bank to reinforce WTO

[28] The UNCED Secretariat estimated in 1992 that in full speed Agenda 21 would require outlays of 625 billion dollars a year, including a transfer from North to South of 125 billion dollars in the form of Official Development Assistance (about 0.7 per cent of the industrialized countries' GNP).

disciplines on developing countries and use WTO sanctions to reinforce IMF/World Bank conditionalities must be resisted' (p. 138).

Several points of the Marrakech agreements should be renegotiated, starting with TRIPS. India should take the initiative for introducing on the agenda of negotiation an international regime on competition policy to control the restrictive business practices of transnational corporations. At the same time, efforts should be made to resist the introduction in WTO of subjects which are best dealt by other organizations of the UN system.

Dubey's views are representative of a large section of informed public opinion in the South. They should be carefully considered if we seriously intend to break the present North–South impasse. In particular, restraint is recommended with respect to the so-called 'social clause'. Independently from the intentions of its proponents, seen from the South, this clause looks as one more instrument of hidden protectionism of the industrial countries.[29]

---

[29] This is not to say that enforcing social standards in developing countries is unimportant. On the contrary, it constitutes a major challenge for the extension and deepening of democracy. However, there are other processes to deal with this question and better forms of assisting social advances in the South, than resorting to discriminatory practices in trade. Abolishing child labour is certainly important. But most children work in agriculture and services and not in export-oriented industries.

In an overview of the debate on the social clause from the Indian perspective, R. Hensman (1996) writes: 'If trade unionists in Europe and North America want to convince us that they are genuinely concerned about these children and not just about their own jobs, they must help us to come up with creative solutions to this problem. Perhaps they could campaign for debt cancellation which is directly set off against government expenditure on rehabilitating and educating these children, and an immediate end to structural adjustment policies which lead to an increase in child labour' (p. 1033).

The Governor of Brasilia, Cristovam Buarque, started an extremely successful programme, which brought back to primary schools fifty thousand children from deprived families, whose parents are getting the equivalent of one minimum wage per month to compensate for the children's forgone income. Several other Brazilian towns have followed this example. An internationally supported programme of fellowships to enable poor children to give up work and go instead to school would do more than blackmailing with the social clause.

The long overdue reform of the Bretton Woods institutions and the streamlining of the WTO are part of a larger problem: that is the reorganization of the entire United Nations system to which the Bretton Woods institutions belong *de jure* but not *de facto*.[30] The South is certainly interested in strengthening and democratizing the United Nations.[31] That does not seem to be the intention of the United States and of the OECD countries, rhetoric notwithstanding. The prospect is worrisome.

Instead, the G-7—a body whose legitimacy is questionable and which speaks only for the Triad—has occupied the void created by the weakness of the UN system. Under its guidance, outright globalization is likely to continue, tempered only by the policies of Nation-States.[32]

Towards New Social Contracts?

A realistic assessment of the present impasse should not distract us from producing a bold vision of the direction in which we want to move.

Democracy is a *foundational value* (A. K. Sen), while markets belong to the instrumental sphere. Perfecting democracy is, to a large extent, synonymous with development redefined in terms of effective appropriation of all human rights by all.

[30] The standard reference on this subject is Stewart Holland's (1994) excellent book.

[31] The South perspective on UN reform has been spelled out in a comprehensive report prepared by the South Centre (1996). The South Centre is a permanent inter-governmental organization of developing countries working distinctly from the Non-Aligned Movement and the Group of 77.

[32] G-7 represents little more than 10 per cent of the world population (Singer, H., 1995). Its enlargement has been suggested (Chavagneux, Ch., 1995), but it would still be a far cry from making it a truly democratic body. A fundamental question to be raised here is that of the relations between the members of the Triad. Will they be able to compromise on their conflicting interests and jointly exercise their condominium on the rest of the world, or, on the contrary, will their contradictions sharpen? In the latter case, conditions would arise, at least for some large countries (China, Russia, India, Brazil), making them practise some kind of 'neo-neutralism' pitching the members of the Triad one against the other.

DECALOGUE OF CITIZEN RIGHTS

1. Professionally assisted birth
2. A safe and secure life space
3. An adequate diet
4. Affordable health care
5. A good, practical education
6. Political participation
7. An economically productive life
8. Protection against unemployment
9. A dignified old age
10. A decent burial

Source: from Friedmann, J. (1996), 'Rethinking Poverty: Empowerment and Citizen Rights', in *International Social Science Journal*, no. 148, June, UNESCO.

In a seminal article, John Friedmann (1996) argues that on the prescriptive level a *new social contract* is needed, based on 'the right to livelihood' and leading to a triangular relationship among State, civil associations and households (the household economy being regarded by him as a centre for the production of livelihood). Friedmann proposes a decalogue of citizen rights (see box above) and suggests that States should commit themselves to honouring these rights before addressing other claims.

In this perspective, then economic growth is no longer regarded as the blind pursuit of growth for its own sake, but as an expansion of the productive forces of society for the purpose of achieving full citizen rights by the entire population. Economic growth thus becomes linked to a specific social goal and requires state intervention into the anarchic play of market forces. The new social contract endows economic theory with a moral purpose, turning it from a utilitarian and excessively individualistic science into a deontological one.

Friedman advocates the empowerment of local communities and considers self-organization of the poor as fundamental for achieving collective survival. But, at the same time, he emphasizes the need for outside help, especially by the State in order to obtain satisfactory results on a scale commensurate with the size of the problem. The voluntary sector cannot by itself cope with it.

'Without direct involvement of the State there can be no escape from massive poverty and disempowerment' (p. 168). He also shows the limitations of 'new localism'. Regional, national and international levels are also involved.[33]

What can be done to bring about this kind of partnership between the civil society and the state? For Friedmann the only hope lies in the launching of political protest movements demanding the transformation of discarded peoples' claims to livelihood in a fundamental human right.

This may prove a realistic assessment of the limitations of less radical approaches. This is not to say, however, that we should not try to put the new social contract on the agenda of political negotiation, supplementing it with a 'natural contract' (Michel Serres, 1990.)

At the same time, we ought to reconstruct the international system on the basis of a *world contract* to be designed along the lines suggested by Riccardo Petrella, the Convenor of the Group of Lisbon (op. cit.) as well as by the Fondation pour le Progrès de l'Homme. Such a contract should at last create conditions for a symmetric *co-development* between South and North prepared by *co-reflexion*, which in spite of the efforts of UNCTAD and other UN bodies did not produce as yet a convincing blueprint of a new North–South compact.[34]

---

[33] See on the same point J. Madrick (op. cit.), p. 162: 'But we cannot expect local government to protect our hard-won civil rights, take care of the poor, or maintain our national defense. Local governments cannot build national highways, oversee far-flung corporations, or even help coordinate an electronic superhighways. Solutions at local levels will play an important role in any renewal of America, but many of the problems that beset us are nationwide in scope. To relinquish some of our most cherished rights to local authorities could be dangerous indeed'.

[34] The 20:20 compact put forward by UNDP addresses only one issue: the social policies. Besides it is open to strong criticism at least on three grounds:

– why 20:20 and not any other figure?

– applying the same ratios to all countries means disregarding their singularities;

– 20 per cent of a rapidly shrinking ODA is a somewhat deceptive goal, as far as the donor countries are concerned.

Whither Europe?

A final comment on this subject is in order here. We have reasons to be proud of our Welfare States and to resist the American way, even though, for reasons explained above, we must recognize the limitations of the social democratic paradigm and look for innovative ways of regaining full employment and moving from *Welfare States* to *caring societies.*

Our attempt should be to 'humanize globalization' which in its present form is 'the law of the jungle', a system in which it is always the rich who make up while the poor get poorer (Guigou, E., 1996). For this, we must succeed in defining a European societal project that could unfold into a world civilizational project.[35] Europe's future will depend on our success or failure in this endeavour, which calls for mobilizing ourselves against the moving force behind globalization: that is 'the world capitalism and his liberal apostles' (Gauron, A., 1996). The European Union runs the risk of becoming the Trojan horse of socially disruptive globalization, if it fails in giving itself a strong common social foundation and, for all practical purposes, limits its ambitions to those of a common market.

Again, as thing stand now, the prospect does not look engaging. Perceptive observers from the other side of the Atlantic consider Europe to be a grand illusion, almost a myth, 'more than a geographical notion but less than an answer to its political and social problems (Judt, T., 1996). According to E. Suleiman (1996) the divorce is total between the real Europe and the mythical and rhetorical one. The discourse is on the social Europe, but the Europe that was built is liberal. 'Notwithstanding the sincere efforts of some eminent Europeans, it is Mrs. Thacher's Europe that got the upper hand.' Capitalism has won. Seen from the South,

[35] 'Pour redonner du sens à la construction européenne-maintenant qu'à l' ouest la paix est acquise, même si ce n'est malheureusement pas le cas dans l'Est de notre continent-, il faut essayer de voir comment l'Europe peut humaniser la mondialisation. Pour cela, il faut réussiz à définir un projet européen de société, il faut que cette démarche soit reprise pour un projet de civilisation à l'échelle mondiale, qui aurait pour ambition, non pas de niveler vers le bas ou d'uniformiser, mais au contraire d'élever vers le haut et de laisser vivre les différences, les diversités et les traditions culturelles, tout en mettant en commun ce sur quoi nous savons nous rassembler' (p. 116).

Europe appears as an inward-looking grouping with highly protectionist agricultural policies and strong neocolonial intersts.[36]
The European left has a long way to go to reverse this situation.

References

Aznar, G. (1996), *Emploi: la grande mutation*, Hachette, Paris.
Bagnasco, A. (1998), *La Costruzzione Sociale del Mercato*, Il Mulino, Bologna.
Bairoch, P. (1996), 'Globalization Myths and realities—One Century of External Trade and Foreign Investment', in Boyer, R. and Drache, D. (eds), *States against Markets—The Limits of Globalization*, Routledge, London and New York.
Bhaduri, A. and Nayyar, D. (1996), *The Intelligent Person's Guide to Liberalization*, Penguin Books, New Delhi.
Brender, A. (1996), *L'impératif de solidarité, la France face à la mondialisation*, La Découverte, Paris.
Broad, R. and Cavanagh, J. (1995–6), 'Don't Neglect the Impoverished South', *Foreign Policy*, no. 101, Winter.
Cardoso, F. H. (1996), 'Os Caminhos da Social Democracia', *Cadernos do PSDB*, nr. 1, Brasilia.
Chavagneux, Ch. (1995), 'L'avenir des institutions de Bretton Woods: Halifax et Après', *Economie Internationale*, n° 64, 4ème trimestre, pp. 3–22.
Cohen, Elie (1996), *La tentation hexagonale, la souveraineté à l'épreuve de la mondialisation*, Fayard, Paris.
Crouch, C. et Streeck, W. (1996), *Capitalismes en Europe*, La Découverte, Paris.
De Bandt, J. et alii (1995), *La France malade du travail*, Bayard Editions, Paris.
Dubey, Muchkund (1996), *An Unequal Treaty—World Trading Order after GATT*, New Age International Limited Publishers, New Delhi.
Ferrer, A. (1996a), 'Desarrollo y Subdesarrollo en un Mundo Global: Los Dilemas de America Latina', IDB Conference on Development Thinking and Practice, Washington, September.
——— (1996b), *Historia de la globalizacion: Origenes del orden economico mundial*, Fondo de Cultura Economica, Buenos Aries.

---

[36] The share of extra-European trade in European GNP does not exceed 10 per cent.

Fitoussi, J. P. et Rosanvallon, P. (1996), *Le nouvel age des inégalites*, Seuil, Paris.

Friedmann, J. (1996), 'Rethinking Poverty: Empowerment and Citizen Rights', *International Social Science Journal*, no. 148, June, UNESCO.

Gauron, A. (1996), 'L'Europe, frein ou accélérateur de la mondialisation', *Apres-demain*, n° 383-4, avril-mai.

Goodland, R. et alii (eds) (1991), *Environmentally Sustainable Economic Development: Building on Brundtland*, UNESCO, Paris.

Guaino, M. (1996), 'Le mythe de la mondialisation, *Le Monde*, 24 Mai.

Guigou, E. (1996), 'L'Europe, une chance d'humaniser la mondialisation', in *Europe, défi de civilisation*, colloque organisé les 2 et 3 février. au Sénat, Paris, par le Forum Alternatives Européennes, pp. 115-120.

Guillebaud, J. C. (1995), *La Trahison des Lumières. Enquête sur le désarroi contemporain*, Editions du Seuil, Paris.

Guimaraes, R. P. (1996), 'Globalizacion, Actores Sociales y Democracia en America Latina', Paper Presented at the Seminar Los Ciudadanos Frente a la Globalizacion, Santiago de Chile, 29-30 mars.

Halimi, S. (1996), 'Economistes en guerre contre les salaires', *La Monde Diplomatique*, juillet.

Haq, M., Kaul, I. and Grunberg, I. (eds) (1996), *The Tobin Tax: Coping with Financial Volatility*, Oxford University Press, Oxford and New York.

Heilbroner, R. and Milberg, W. (1995), *The Crisis of Vision in Modern Economic Thought*, Cambridge University Press, Cambridge and New York.

Hensman, R. (1996), 'Minimum Labour Standards and Trade Agreements —An Overview of the Debate', *Economic and Political Weekly*, 20-7 April.

Hirst, P. and Thompson, G. (1996), *Globalization in Question*, Polity Press/Blackwell, Cambridge (UK).

Hobsbawm, E. (1994), *The Age of Extremes—A History of the World, 1914-91*, Pantheon Books, New York.

Holland, S. (1994), *Towards a New Bretton Woods: Alternatives for the Global Economy*, Spokesman, Nottingham.

Ianni, O. (1995), *Teorias da Globalização*, Civilização Brasileira, Rio de Janeiro.

Judt, T. (1996), 'Europe: The Grand Illusion', *The New York Review of Books*. 11 July, p. 6.

Kapstein, E. B. (1996), 'Workers and the World Economy', *Foreign Affairs*, May/June, vol. 45.

Kothari, R. (1993), *Growing Amnesia. An Essay on Poverty and the Human Consciousness*, Viking/Penguin Books, New Delhi.

Krugman, P. (1994), *Peddling Prosperity*, W. W. Norton, New York.

Meda, D. (1995), *Le travail, une valeur en voie de disparition*, Autier, Paris.
Miringoff, M. L., Miringoff, M. and Opdycke, S. (1996), 'The Growing Gap between Standard Economic Indicators and the Nation's Social Health', *Challenge*, July–August.
Naisbitt, J. (1995), *Global Paradox*, Avon Books, New York.
Nations, Unies (1995), *Déclaraction et Programme d'action de Copenhague*, Sommet mondial pour le développement social, New York.
Nayyar, D. (1995), 'Globalisation: the Past in Our Present', Presidential Address, Indian Economic Association, Chandigarh, 21–30 December.
Ohmae, K. (1996), *The End of the Nation-State*, traduit en francais sous le titre *De l'Etat-Nation aux Etats-Regions*, Dunod, Paris.
Phelps, E. S. (1996), Interview, *Le Monde*, 12 mars.
Rachline, F. (1996), *Services publics, Economie de Marché*, Presses de la Foundation Nationale des Sciences politiques, Paris.
Rifkin, J. (1995), *The End of Work: the Decline of the Global Labor Force and the Dawn of the Post-Market Era*, Tracher/Putnam, New York.
Roustang, G. et al. (1996), *Vers un nouveau contrat social*, Desclée de Brouwer, Paris.
Sachs, I. (1980), 'Times-spaces of Development', *Diogenes*, nr. 112, pp. 75–90, Paris.
——— (1993), *Transition Strategies towards the 21st Century*, Interest Publications for Research and Information System for the Non-Aligned and Other Development Countries, New Delhi, p. 92.
——— (1994b), Population, développement et emploi, *Revue Internationale des Sciences Sociales*, n° 141 ('Population: problèmes et politiques'), September, pp. 409–26, Paris.
——— (1995a) *Searching for New Development Strategies: the Challenges of Social Summit*, Paper Prepared on the Occasion of the World Summit for Social Development, Copenhagen, 6–12 March, UNESCO, Paris: p. 48 (MOST Policy Papers, 1).
——— (1995b), 'The Quantitative and Qualitative Measurement of Development—Its Implications and Limitations', *International Social Science Journal*, no. 143, March.
——— (1996), Growth with Dedevelopment—A comment on Gert Rosenthal's paper, IDB Conference on Development Thinking and Practice, Washington, September.
Sachs, I. and Gowariker, Vasant (1994a), 'Redefining the Good Society: A North–South Dialogue on Challenges of 21st Century', *Economic and Political Weekly*, 4 June, pp. 1383–5.
Séguin, Ph. (1996), *En attendant l'emploi...*, Seuil, Paris.

Serres, M. (1990), *Le contrat naturel*, François Bourin, Paris.

Sing, A. (1996), 'Catching up with the West: A Perspective on Asian Economic Development', IDB Conference on Development Thinking and Practice, Washington, September.

Singer, H. W. (1995), 'Revitalizing the United Nations: Five Proposal', *IDS Bulletin*, vol. 26, no. 4, pp. 35–9.

Soros, G. (1996) Interview, *Veja*, May 1, pp. 6–10.

South Centre (1996a), 'Liberalization and Globalization: the Issues at the Stake for the South and for UNCTAD'.

Streeten, P. (1996), 'Globalisation and Competitiveness: What are the Implications for Development Thinking and Practice?' IDB Conference on Development Thinking and Practice, Washington, September.

Suleiman, E. (1996), 'Europe et capitalisme', *Le monde*, 18 avril.

Sunkel, O. (ed.) (1993), *Development from Within: Toward a Neostructuralist Approach for Latin America*, Lynne Reinner Publishers, Boulder.

Tinbergen, Jan et al. (coordinators) (1976), *Reshaping the International Order, A Report to The Club of Rome*, E. P. Dutton & Co., New York.

Tomorrow's World, William Morrow and Co., New York.

UNCTAD (1996), 'Globalization and Liberalization, Development in the Face of Two Powerful Current Reports of the Secretary-General of UNCTAD, Rubens Ricupero, to the Ninth Session of the Conference.

UNDP (1996), *Human Development Report 1996*, New York.

Appendix 1
Work, a Vanishing Value?

In France, the transformation of work into autonomous 'activities' has been a major concern for Jacques Robin, editor of *Transversales Science/ Culture* and the movement *Europe 99*. In the United States, Jeremy Rifkin's (1995) book, significantly titled, *The End of Work*, attracted the attention of the media. It also influenced the thinking of Philippe Séguin (1996). Rifkin sees the emergence of a two-gear society: a small professional knowledge sector, highly educated, the top 20 per cent of the workforce, on the one side, and, on the other side, the 80 per cent in dead-end and temporary jobs, underemployed and unemployed. While his analysis is correct, his concept of third volunteer sector is unconvincing because it fails to explain how this sector will be financed. Rifkin's ideas are close to those of the French proponents of *économie solidaire* and *économie plurielle* (see e.g. Roustang, G. et alii, 1996).

Another controversial concept is that of a universal tax-free citizen income propagated by the Basic Income European Network (BIEN) and, lately endorsed in the UK by a commission chaired by Lord Dahrendorf (*The Economist*, 27 April 1996) In France, the journal *MAUSS* (1996) has published a voluminous dossier edited by A. Caillé. While recognizing the generous intentions of the proponents of the guaranteed income, I cannot accept it for reasons that have been well stated by A. Gorz (1994): work confers economic citizenship. While the abolition of the microsocial and private spheres leads to the subordination of the individual, a life without work universally exchangeable means that he is condemned to uselessness and public inexistence. Guy Aznar (1996) fears that the guaranteed income would legitimize once for ever the dual society. Fitoussi and Rosanvallon (1996) take a similar stand.

In my paper *Les temps/espaces du développement* published in 1980, I have argued that the 'surplus' of time released from heteronomous work is the measure of cultural freedom, just like the economic surplus is the measure of economic freedom.

As for the current debate, my position coincides with the stance taken by Guy Aznar (1996, pp. 132–3):

La mutation du travail à laquelle nous assistons ne nous conduit pas à sa disparition mais au contraire à sa réinvention. Plus que jamais il apparaît que le travail constitue une caracteristique essentielle de l'homme,présentant un caractère anthropologique et conditionnant l'expression de l'identité humaine. Le travail permet à l'homme de se relier au monde et de se relier aux autres, en instituant un mécanisme d'échange économique, affectif et social, alors que l'impossibilité d'accéder au travail constitue une forme de bannissement de la société, une exclusion du monde.

Contrary to those who affirm, like Dominique Meda (1995), that work is a vanishing value, Aznar considers that work as value will be *reinvented* and will conquer new spaces.

This philosophical discussion should not distract us from the urgency of a more pedestrian approach: increasing productive investment! (see de Bandt et alii, 1996). For this it is essential to curb financial speculation.

Appendix 2

A Note on Employment-generating Development Strategies

1. To avoid any misunderstanding, increases in labour productivity are, as such, a bounty—they provide the ultimate basis for economic progress (more goods, less working time or a combination of both). The issue at stake is, how is this progress managed and shared? To whom do the additional goods accrue? Who benefits from the reduction of working time and who becomes its victim, and is excluded from the workforce?

2. Given the present trends in technical progress, reduction of employment cannot be avoided in industries turning out tradeables and modern services. However, the boundary between tradeables and non-tradeables is not fixed once for ever. It depends on the degree of openness of an economy and the form of its insertion in the world market. Moreover, through cross-subsidies it is possible to ensure the survival of some highly labour-intensive cottage and small-scale industries.

3. The trend towards substitution of labour by capital is magnified in many countries by policy mistakes consisting of subsidization of capital, overburdening of labour costs with social overheads (which should be financed out of value added tax), overvaluation of currency (which lowers the costs of imported capital goods) and fiscal measures favouring accelerated substitution of equipment (instead of slowing down the rate of real depreciation).

4. Shrinking of employment in some sectors must be compensated with the expansion of other sectors which can still absorb labour, either in the form of wage jobs or through self-employment, particularly in agriculture through family peasant farming. *Industrialization without depeasantization* (Ismail Sabri Abdallah) is probably the only viable option for densely populated countries and an opportunity for those Latin American and African countries, which still have large reserves of agricultural land.

Sectors enjoying high rates of increase in productivity of labour should be put to contribution through appropriate fiscal policies (taxing of capital equipment) to finance the expansion of the labour absorbing sectors.

5. Environmental considerations point to the objective of seeking a higher productivity for energy and other natural resources (e.g. increasing the number of kilometres per litre of fuel or the yield of grain per cubic meter of irrigated water). This can be achieved by energy, water and resource conservation, waste and materials recycling and reuse, as well as by extending through improved maintenance the lifecycle of existing infrastructures, built environment, equipment and vehicles.

As a matter of fact, environmental, economic and social criteria coincide in such 'triple-win' activities which are often labour-intensive and at the macro-economic level (though not necessarily in micro-economic terms) finance themselves, at least partly, by the resultant saving of resources and foregoing or postponing of reposition investment. Local agendas 21, urabn and rural, should be mainly concerned with the identification and implementation of such 'triple-win' projects for which the State should provide the necessary support in the form of appropriate credit lines, service and purchase contracts, research and technical assistance. This is an area for innovative experiments in partnerships between public sector, private enterprises, workers, service cooperatives, citizen movements and organizations.

Although the employment potential of the activities described above may vary considerably from place to place, there are reasons to believe that it is quite considerable, the more so that it does not require significant additional investment.

6. Given the prohibitive cost of urbanization of rural migrants in terms of infrastructure, housing and job provision, all the possibilities of less capital intensive rural development should be carefully ascertained. They include:

- the modernization of family farms by applying science-intensive, resource saving and labour absorbing technologies of the second green revolution;

- the settlement of landless peasants through land reforms and colonization schemes;

- promotion of bio-energies;

- decentralized industrialization;

- production of services for the population.

While the expectation of one billion jobs in ten years (Swaminathan) may be too optimistic, this is by far the single most important reserve for employment creation and a key element in the pursuit of food security.

7. Public works allow more scope for choosing appropriate technologies than market-oriented activities. Their volume depends on the ability to generate public savings.

8. In all countries, including the industrial ones, the potential demand for social services is far greater than the current output, limited by lack of adequate funding. Progress in this area will depend on the capacity to design less costly service delivery systems based on partnerships involving the State, the users, the citizen organizations (the private non-profit sector) and the private enterprises. In developing countries where the wages are low, special attention should be given to *qualified labour-intensive* delivery systems, the unit cost of such services being much lower there than in the advanced countries. This comparative advantage should lead to an inversion of historical sequence followed by the industrial countries and expanding social services without waiting to become rich. China, Cuba, but also Sri Lanka and Kerala (a state in south India) provide strong arguments in favour of such an approach.

9. The points 2 to 8 of this note constitute a checklist of questions providing an entry-point in the process of formulating an employment-oriented development strategy. This preliminary identification of employment possibilities should be further redefined by analysing the policies on which they are predicated and ascertaining the macroeconomic balances. Planning is always an iterative process. But *the entry-point matters*. That is why the practice of ILO-sponsored country reports on employment, which yielded significant results in the seventies, should be revived.

Appendix 3

Whither 'Mixed Economies'? (West, East, South)

Insofar as dogmatic neoliberalism is a poor and dangerous substitute for dogmatic central planning and patrimonial statism, both Eastern European and developing countries should be encouraged and helped in searching new institutional settings belonging to the broad category of 'mixed economies'.

There is, therefore, an urgent need for going beyond the simplified description of such economies in terms of a juxtaposition of market place and planning (as much market as possible, as little planning as necessary, some would say).

One should aim at building a typology of the diverse existing and plausible forms of articulation between the private, the public and the social sectors (the latter consisting of cooperatives, mutual aid institutions and citizen associations), as well as the household non-market economy. The different forms of articulation between the local, national and transnational spaces of development should be likewise considered (in P. Streeten's terminology macro-macro, macro, meso, micro and micro-micro levels).

The description of the institutional settings should be supplemented by an analysis of the forms of regulation of mixed economies, of the range of incentive systems and policy instruments and of the adjustment and reforms paths, leading from the present state to the desired institutional pattern.

The proposed transition paths should be subject to the three criteria of social equity, ecological prudence and economic efficiency. Such solutions to the present crisis, capable of minimizing the social and ecological costs, are far from evident, and may even require counter-intuitive measures in their initial stages (e.g. rationing as a way of protecting the vulnerable strata of the population during the transition to a balanced market economy).

Hence the need for a comparative institutional analysis of 'mixed economies', as they exist, or have existed in industrialized and developing countries, as well as in Eastern Europe during the years 1944–8.

Considerable literature on the subject has piled up since the formulation of this proposal in November 1989. Yet, there is still room for a comparative critical synthesis. The research field should be now extended to the actual experience of post-socialist countries and to an assessment of the impact of liberalization reforms in the developing countries.

5

People's Livelihoods in the Real Economy

The two years that have elapsed since the Copenhagen meeting did not contribute much to dispel the concern and gloom over the dismal social predicament affecting a sizeable segment (if not the majority) of the world population. Our technology and profit-driven economies follow their course characterized by modest rates of almost jobless growth, profligate and environmentally disruptive patterns of energy and resource use, an increasingly skewed income distribution between and inside nations and, last but not the least, by massive relegation of redundant working force to the 'concentration camps of forced idleness'[1] and the ensuing social exclusion. Their hands and minds are not needed anymore by the rich and powerful; robots are more productive.

In this way non-exploitation becomes an even greater evil for the excluded than outright exploitation, the former reinforcing the latter through the swelling of the global labour reserve army and the delocalization of relatively more labour-intensive activities to low-income countries. Of all the forms of wastefulness in which our civilization excels, this is perhaps the worst, as nothing can make up for wasted lives and forgone opportunities for human self-realization.

It is only natural that the increased labour productivity resulting from technical progress should bring about a reduction of global

[1] I borrow this metaphor from the Italian novelist Carlo Levi.

demand for work, thus creating conditions for freeing people's time for other more rewarding activities and allowing for pluralistic lifestyles, the ascent of *homo ludens* at the expenses of *homo faber* (see Sachs, 1987). However, this kind of social progress requires that both, the total demand for work and the product derived from it, are equitably shared among the entire labour force through appropriate planning, regulation of working-time and income policies. Needless to say we are very distant from this goal. What is worse, under the spell of neoliberal gospel we are drifting away from it towards income, wealth and employment concentrating growth with social dedevelopment.[2]

This dismal trend prevails with a few exceptions in all the three groups of countries: the industrialized, the post-Soviet and the so-called developing ones including the United States whose much publicized positive record in employment generation, as compared with Europe, owes much to statistical jugglery.[3]

Political manipulation of employment statistics is not an exclusive privilege of the United States. In the already quoted article Joseph Fitchett reports that the Conservative Party in Britain had altered unemployment definitions more than 30 times, each time reducing the number of jobless people. In France, three different measures of unemployment are used at present.

More fundamentally, the very concepts of wage jobs, labour markets and rates of unemployment derived from situations prevailing in the enterprise world of industrialized market economies cannot be extended to less developed economies, where only

[2] Note: In Paul Streeten's terms (1997), these are exclusive forms of growth 'jobless, voiceless, ruthless and futureless' (the latter on account of unsustainability).

[3] Official unemployment statistics in the United States do not include the working-age men out of work because they are in prison or on parole. The 1.5 million incarcerated men and the 8.1 million on parole represent nearly 10 per cent of the male work force. According to Richard Freeman of Harvard University, including these numbers, adjusted for those on paroles with jobs, would lift the unemployment rate of about 5 per cent into double digits, comparable with the rate of 12 per cent in the European Union (quoted by Joseph Fitchett in *International Herald Tribune*, July 2, 1997). Leslie Thurow (1995) estimated that underemployment and unemployment rates would be at least 15 per cent of the American Workforce. For the enthusiasts of the American model, let it be said that the crime rate in the United States is ten times more than in Western Europe.

a fraction of work force is employed in this way. The Indian example, by no means unique, is quite instructive in this respect. According to *the Statistical Outline of India, 1996–7*, India had in 1991 a total population of 846.3 million people (74.3 per cent rural), out of which 278.9 million were workers classified as 'main' and another 27.1 million as 'marginal'. Among the main workers 38.4 per cent were cultivators and another 26.4 per cent agricultural labourers. Manufacturing and processing industries employed only 10.2 per cent of the workers, out of which 2.4 per cent are in household industry. Even more telling are the figures relative to employment in 'organized sector', i.e. all establishments in public sector and all non-agricultural establishments in private sector employing 10 or more persons: in 1991 only 19.06 million people were employed in the public sector and 7.68 million in the organized private sector, altogether less than 10 per cent of the workforce. Less than one Indian in a hundred was employed by private organized modern enterprises defined through the unsatisfactory criterion of the number of employees.[4]

No wonder that several developing countries demagogically boast of rates of open joblessness that are considerably lower than those of industrialized countries helped in this by the complacency of ILO, which recommends the same analytical categories to all countries, irrespective of their socio-economic structure and of the extension of disguised unemployment and underemployment. Further complications arise from considering those earning wages inferior to the poverty line as underemployed.

Considerable complexity is involved in estimating the degree of underutilization of labour potential within peasant family farms taking into consideration such factors like the seasonal variations of demand for work, the different capabilities of gender and age groups, the specific rationality of peasant farming and the moral economy prevailing inside the household. They do not yield themselves easily to synthetic indicators of unemployment equivalent.

[4] The number of employees does not discriminate between small-scale technically backward cottage (artisanal) and modern industries, not to speak of individual consultants and small businesses operating in the cyberspace. Let it be also recalled that cottage industries requiring a low capital labour coefficient often have a high capital-output ratio, on account of very low labour productivity.

Even greater is the dearth of data about the disguised unemployment and underemployment in the unorganized urban economy, as well as the labour conditions and income distribution prevailing there. This is so because the governments do not care about producing these data. It is far more convenient to pretend that the so-called 'informal economy' evades systematic statistical coverage and to treat it as a residual category: encompassing all the economic activities that happen outside the organized sector and supposedly employing all those who are neither employed in the organized sector nor registered as unemployed! In this way the gravity of the unemployment problem is assumed away, even though it could be ascertained by confronting the figures of the new entrants in the workforce, calculated from demographic data, with the number of additional jobs created.[5] Furthermore, the less satisfactory the social security net for the unemployed, the greater the chance that jobless people will not care to be registered as such, reducing in this way the statistics of the openly unemployed.

Official data about unemployment are thus underestimated, while those about employment seem overestimated by exaggerating the number of jobs created in the informal sector.

According to ILO estimates,[6] quoted in our ECLAC study, out of every 100 new jobs created in Latin America between 1990 and 1995, 84 were in the informal sector, in which 56 per cent of all the regions's workers are occupied. On average they earn half the amount paid in modern enterprises (not speaking of lack of social protection).

In Africa, the preponderance of the informal sector is even greater. According to a UN report, it accounts for 62.5 per cent of the urban labour force and 25 per cent of the total labour force

---

[5] According to *O Estado de São Paulo* of 16 June 1997, Brazil (with a working population of 74 million) should create 2 million jobs per year to accommodate the new entrants to the labour market and to take care of the backlog of unemployed. Instead it generates 600 thousand new formal jobs (in 1996 there were 7.3 million dismissals and 7.9 million admittances). This enormous deficit accumulating year after year is not properly reflected in the official statistics of unemployment. According to ECLAC, urban unemployment in six largest metropolitan areas in Brazil was in 1996 as low as 5.7 per cent.

[6] Quoted in *CEPAL News*, vol. XVII, no. 6 June 1997.

in low-income Africa, contributing 20 per cent of GDP. During the eighties it absorbed 19 million people while the formal sector provided only 2 million new jobs. In the present decade the informal sector is expected to perform the role of 'the most important labour sponge (sic!) in Africa's labour markets where it will provide some 60 to 70 per cent of the job openings' (p. 5).

The report sees in the informal sector a source of vitality for African economies, bound to last for many years, commendable, as described in the memorable ILO report on Kenya (1972) by the ease to entry, reliance on indigenous resources, family ownership of enterprises, small-scale operation, labour-intensive technology, skills acquired outside the formal school system, unregulated and competitive markets. The authors conclude by an exhortation of African countries to

look forward to utilizing the informal sector as a source of creativity and entrepreneurial spirit, and a breeding ground for a work ethic of redefined self-reliance that can eventually constitute a firm basis for sustainable development (p. 48).

They go as far as to state:

The potential of the informal sector could be harnessed to become the core of an integrated African economy, the hub of technology development and industrialization and a fertile ground for the acquisition of entrepreneurial skills (ibidem).

A very tall order indeed, when confronted with the extremely low levels of productivity aided income prevailing in the informal sector, half of which consists of small-scale commercial activities assumed mainly by women.

The 'Informal Economy': A Solution or a Problem?

Faced by the dismal prospect of jobless growth, governments, international organizations and many scholars make a virtue of necessity, turning their hopes to the 'informal sector' as an alleged solution to growing unemployment and underemployment.

But, at the same time, by functioning outside the realm of public regulation, the 'informal sector' creates severe social, economic and environmental problems, insofar as moonlighting and informal commercial and industrial activities result in massive tax evasion and unfair competition with organized business, while depriving the workers and operators in this sector of social and legal protection, as well as of access to public services and organized banking.

Informality often leads to abject exploitation in sweatshops, exceedingly high rentals for miserable dwellings in slums, real estate transactions with no right to legal property title, all sorts of exactions from casual farm workers, blatantly inequitable terms of trade imposed on farmers and forest people, etc. It also implies higher operational and living costs, e.g. by being compelled to resort to money lenders instead of banks or to buy electrical power and water from middlemen who control access to the public sources of provisioning.

Needless to say, environmental protection is not much of a concern to the operators of informal business, even though some of these may be engaged in waste disposal and recycling.

Finance ministers have their reasons to complain about tax evasion. The informal activities encompass a myriad of small-scale undertakings and individual autonomous workers who could be tax-exempted without much loss to the treasury (and probably ought to be). But they also include fairly large operations generating huge profits, concentrated in the hands of wealthy people if not millionaires (not to speak of the operation of the illegal economy).

The informal sector is sometimes described in almost romantic terms as the locus of solidarity and conviviality. But the two only go together whenever the poor and the excluded manage to organize themselves to revive the age-old practices of self-help and collective action. Commendable as it may be, this is not by means the general case. The spread of the ideology of exacerbated individualism and of social Darwinism works in the opposite direction. Informal markets are often ruthless.

But it is time to clear some conceptual problems, starting by defining the borderlines of the 'informal economy'.

Informal Sector or Informal Activities?

Uncle, I shall take care of your car while you go to restaurant.' The self-appointed parking car-taker, often a child, expects from you a modest reward in cash and, hopefully, in smaller Brazilian towns, the meal left-overs wrapped for you by the waiter. You better accept the deal if you don't want to find your tyres flat.

Is this boy working, begging or blackmailing you? What to say of the five-year olds who live dangerously selling chewing gum or cleaning the front-windows while your car is stopped on a traffic light? And of the Parisian homeless people who propose to subway passengers yet another copy of one of the many magazines published by their association?

Sometimes, the distinction is difficult to draw between informal economic activities and asking for as charity.

At the other extreme lies the blurred frontier between illegal but tolerated and frankly criminal activities with all the shades in between:

- vending in the streets sundry goods, fruits, homemade sweets and ice-cream without being licensed;

- peddling counterfeit watches or smuggled cigarettes;

- going into prostitution and petty theft;

- participating in narco-traffic, illegal gambling and criminal gangs.

A recent UN report estimated in 400 billion dollars the annual turnover of narco-traffic, the equivalent of 8 per cent of world trade.

How many people are involved in it? According to an official estimate (*Veja*, 25 June 1997) in Rio de Janeiro metropolitan area alone, out of a population of about ten million people, they numbered 150 thousand, engaged in different capacities and, in many cases, on a part-time basis. The number of people whose life is affected by the narco-traffic is much greater, as rival gangs control *manu militari* different favelas (shantytowns).

The attitude of the population towards them is ambivalent. They are feared because they are quick at pushing their guns. But, at the same time, they provide jobs, spend considerable amounts of money and, in the absence of the State, whose legal representatives do not dare penetrating the drug dealers' strongholds, they engage in clientelistic welfare practices assisting the disabled, give presents to all newly wed couples and Christmas gifts to all kids.

'Our king is dead', chanted a several thousand strong crowd mourning a drugdealer who died in a helicopter crash while trying to escape from a high-security prison. They descended from the favela from which the man commanded his operations. To the people of this favela he was a benefactor. Police had to intervene to prevent them from building a monument in his memory.

This episode underscores the complexity of real social and economic configurations in which people live and function, the more so that many inhabitants of the favela are regularly employed in 'formal' businesses located downtown, or else work as domestic employees for middle-class households. In what follows, we shall exclude from our considerations the criminal sector, insisting once more on the fact that the criteria of legality/illegality and the sanctions for their transgression vary from country to country and may change over time.[7]

The dichotomy 'formal/informal' does not render the complexity of actual situations. At any rate, the opposition between the formal and informal sectors is a misrepresentation insofar as it implies the existence of distinct economic circuits functioning apart. We ought to speak instead of informal activities intermingled with the formal ones in a variety of configurations. A few examples follow:

Doppio Lavoro (double work). Moonlighting in Italy was studied under this name by a team of sociologists led by Luciano Gallino. If you are not good at do-it-yourself (or busy or lazy) and you wish to save on value added tax and social and commercial overheads, instead of calling an enterprise you will informally contract the services of a plumber to fix your bathroom or a painter to refresh your flat. They will be happy to make some extra-money (not taxed) by working on weekends, holidays or after office hours. Illegal? Yes. But widespread and tolerated, at least so long as the paint has not been stolen from the enterprise in which the painter works (it was quite common in the 'second economy' in the Soviet world where getting the paint on the market was often impossible).

The second job may be quite different from the first one.

In Ilheus in Northeast Brazil, I came across a biology teacher-cum-taxi driver! In socialist Poland, notoriously short of taxis, drivers of official cars were happy to give you a lift against a nice tip.

[7] The so-called 'black economy' was severely repressed under Stalinism, but progressively came to be tolerated, at least in countries like Hungary or Poland long before real socialism collapsed. Likewise, the 'economia sommersa' (hidden economy) in Italy is a misnomer, as it functions in the open.

In the examples just given the same people participate in formal and informal activities. It happens equally with enterprises.

In February 1997 the Italian police raided leather workshops in Milan, Florence and parts of Tuscany, confiscating thousands of bags with brand names like Chanel, Prada and Dior and marked for export to Spain, Switzerland and Japan. The bags were not cheap rip-offs. Many were indistinguishable from the genuine article. And for good reason. The same craftsmen who stitched together the originals for the luxury market were in many cases selling bootleg copies on the side (*International Herald Tribune*, July 4, 1997).

That is how the Italian *economia sommersa* works, expert at producing counterfeit luxury goods, to make a fast tax-free buck. Experts estimate the size of this illegal commerce at 6 billion dollars a year, probably an underestimate.

Another variation, illustrated below, on the theme of the formal/informal mix linked with globalization, is related to the proliferation of sweatshops in the international capital market.

99 per cent Perspiration. Under this title, *The Economist* described on June 21st, 1997, the working in Honduras of the 11 industrial parks-in effect free-trade zones-housing 155 clothing industries, many owned by South Koreans and exporting to the United States thanks to the Caribbean Basin Initiative. South Korean manufacturers move to Honduras attracted by the access to American markets, low wages and rents, tax breaks and easy repatriation of profits. These are tough employers indeed. In the worst sweatshops women work 16 hour days with a single half-hour break. Some work 80 hours a week without overtime pay or take work home at night and at weekends to fulfil their quotas. Women are sometimes summarily sacked if they get pregnant or join trade unions. They are paid 29 American cents an hour.

In Vietnam the government blamed foreign investors' labour practices—low pay, long hours and excessive production targets—for strikes in shoe factories owned by South Korean and Taiwan contractors working for the US sportswear giant Nike (*International Herald Tribune*, July 4, 1997).

Capitalism always knew how to subordinate precapitalist forms of production in order to take advantage of them. In the same way, the formal economy benefits from the informal activities which blossom under the pressure of two totally opposed forces:

– on the one hand, the last chance survival strategies of all those who are not included in the formal economy or were excluded from it;[8]

– on the other hand, the practices of those who seek personal advantages by subverting the established economic and legal order stopping short of outright criminal acts.

As pointed out by Saskia Sassen in the Habitat II Dialogue on the Future of Urban Employment in Istanbul, in many of the cities of the developing and developed countries informal activities are very much part of the mainstream market economy (ILO, 1997). To the extent to which expansion of international trade will not spread across the world more jobs and higher wages, but rather result in sharper competition, more inequalities and further divergence between highly paid specialized jobs and low-skilled, low-wage jobs, the prospect is for more informal employment, not as a path to development but as a symptom of misdevelopment.

We are thus in presence of a *formal–informal continuum or web* as rightly observed in a survey of informal businesses in Rio de Janeiro (IBASE/SEBRAE, 1997, p. 16). The dichotomous opposition of formal and informal economy, yet another *avatar* of primitive dualism, does not correspond to reality. Nor is it true, alas, that the informal activities provide the much needed opportunity to earn meagre livelihood to the unemployed. More often, they result in extra income to those who are employed, leaving the excluded to their predicament. This observation is important, insofar as it undermines the assertion that the informal sector absorbs the surplus work force like a 'sponge'.

According to the neoliberal gospel, so long as the redundant working hands don't register as unemployed and people don't starve to death in the streets, the situation is under control

[8] We find there three categories of people:

– those uprooted from their traditional settings who did not yet qualify to the modern economy (the refugees from the countryside awaiting their urbanization in the shantytowns),

– those expelled from the modern economy through downsizing;

– those already born and brought up in the cities anxiously waiting for the first decent job opportunity.

thanks to the providential action of the market forces which rule over the informal activities. The responsibility of the State is disengagement. The less it intervenes, the better it is, as the State's heavy and corrupt bureaucracy obstructs the efforts of dynamic informal entrepreneurs, many of whom have the stuff to become new Morgans and Rockfellers.[9] Factual evidence suggests a completely different stance.

Public action is necessary to support the informal activities deemed positive and to assist their progressive inclusion into the formal economy while curbing the negative ones. For this, as postulated in the ILO report on the Istanbul dialogue, we should proceed to deconstruct this highly heterogenous concept, whose fuzziness is attested by the multiplicity of definitions and adjectives used to describe it (informal, unorganized, unofficial, unrecorded, shadow, second, subterranean, black, etc.).[10]

Before turning to this task we shall replace the informal activities in a broader analytical framework addressing the 'real economy' as a whole, so as to also include the non-market household economy which should not be confused with informal market activities.[11]

[9] This argument has been developed in the much publicized book on Peru by Hernan de Soto (1986), an apology for the virtues of the informal sector and an outright condemnation of public intervention. Hernan de Soto has since changed his stance. He now recognizes that it pays to operate in the official economy rather than to stay informal, even though the cost of 'formalization' is prohibitive (a point well taken). He therefore recommends public action to regularize informal properties, starting by real estate and housing. He estimates informal private properties in Peru at 70 billion dollars. Up to now de Soto's action succeeded in legalizing 350,000 informal properties, about 10 per cent of the total and 260,000 enterprises. According to de Soto, as many as 70 per cent of Peruvians function informally (interview to *Veja*, 19 March 1997).

[10] For an excellent review article of the different definitions, see Portes, A., (1994). See also Archambault and Greffe (eds) (1984) and Lautier, B. (1994).

[11] E. von Weizsäcker, A. B. Lovins and L. H. Lovins (1997) broadened the concept of the informal sector to encompass all human activities, economic and non-economic, situated outside the money economy. This is somewhat confusing. I certainly agree with them that 'sleeping, eating, loving and bringing up children are not subordinate activities we could do without, but the indispensable foundation of all human existence' (p. 295). But I do not see why they should be included in the 'informal sector'.

Real Economy: Concept and Analytical Framework[12]

The 'real' economy can be seen as a lattice of segmented yet interconnected labour and product markets and non-markets (see Fig. 5.1). The two basic labour-product configurations are: the commoditized economy and the non-market household economy (arrows 1a and 2a).

Now, side by side with the organized sector of the commoditized economy, operated by enterprises—large and small, public and private—complying with all the legal, fiscal and administrative regulations of the labour and product markets, there exist several 'informal' markets (arrow 1b) which can be classified according to their degree of illegality, ranging down to the crime syndicates. Another segment of the labour market, usually included in the definition of the informal sector, is the group of self-employed (arrow 4); strictly speaking the latter are not on the labour market; however, the produce of their work comes to the product market.

In contrast to the commoditized economy, household activities are situated both outside the labour and the product markets (arrow 2a), although the total household consumption consists of goods and services purchased on the market in addition to the self-produced ones.

It is difficult to estimate the value of household production in monetary terms, as imputation to family work of wages prevailing on the market constitutes an obvious overestimate. Estimates of time spent on in household chores are more reliable. For example, the household unpaid labour of women in Finland took 288 minutes per day in 1980 and 236 minutes in 1990. For men the corresponding figures were 114 and 140 (Pietila, H. 1997, p. 116–7).[13]

[12] This section is partly based on an earlier paper by the author (Sachs, 1988a).

[13] The Finnish estimates put the value of unpaid household work as high as 42.9 per cent of GDP. Using the same kind of flawed methodology UNDP in its *Human Development Report 1995* estimated in 16 billion dollars the amount of unpaid or underpaid women's labour. Out of that 11 trillion is the non-monetized contribution of women, as compared to a world GDP of 23 trillion dollars. Of the total burden of work, women carry on average 53 per cent in developing countries and 51 per cent in industrial countries. Out of the total time of women's work only one-third is paid, while men get paid for three-fourths of their working time.

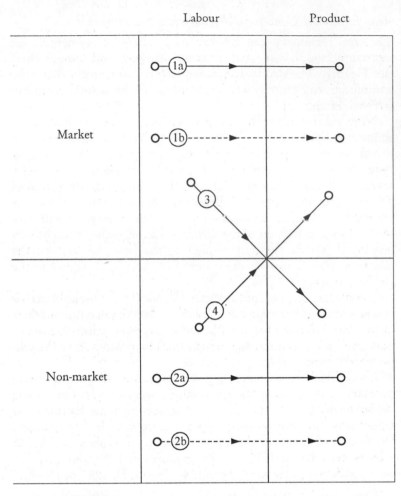

Fig. 5.1 Classification of sectors of the real economy according to whether labour and product pass through markets formally or informally

1a Commoditized sector (wage labour, product sold on the market)
1b Informal markets
2a Household sector (labour and product do not pass through the market)
2b Social sector (collective non-market production) and quasi-markets
3 Public sector (wage labour, product distributed freely)
4 Petty commodity economy (self-employed producers, marketed product)

It is reasonable to assume that household activities take about half of the working time in industrial societies.

The non-market segment of the economy comprises in addition the social sector (arrow 2b) consisting of all collective activities organized outside the market by neighbourhood and community groups, citizens associations, etc. Their common trait is that they are governed, just like the household sector, by rules of moral economy and not by a market-oriented economic rationality.

A natural extension of the social sector are the 'quasi-markets', i.e. local exchange arrangements functioning without money.

For sake of completeness, we ought to mention the public sector (arrow 3) providing free goods and services, which are produced by public servants who earn wages just like the workers of the commoditized sector.

The lattice of the real economy provides a suitable framework to address the question of choice configurations open to individuals, households or extended families with respect to the allocation of their time and incomes and the resulting consumption and life-style patterns. This is the subject-matter of an anthropological economy unfolding into a generalized consumption theory, in which consumption is simultaneously described in terms of bundles of goods and services purchased on the markets and/or self-produced, as well as in terms of patterns of time-use.

Two equally reductionist temptations must be avoided: putting a price tag to time, and reasoning exclusively in terms of time allocation.

We shall, however, use the latter as an entry-point.

Four choice configurations are theoretically open to, whatever the case, the individual, or the household of the extended family (see Fig. 5.2):

– allocation of time for economic and non-economic activities;

– apportionment of time of economic activities between market and non-market;

– apportionment of time devoted to market activities between the formal and the informal markets;

– apportionment of time outside the market between the household and the social sectors.

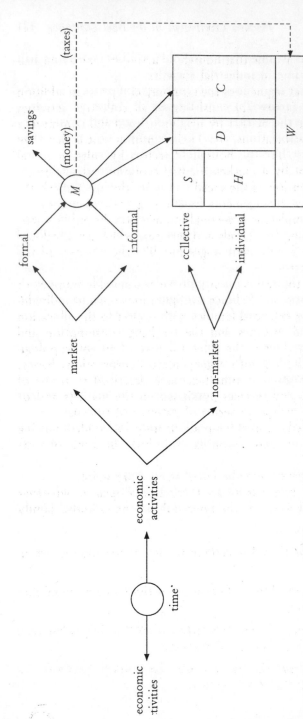

Fig. 5.2 Structure of everyday life: time allocation and consumption patterns

Notes: 'Box' diagram shows goods and services consumed.

C—Consumer goods and services purchased through the market.

D—Durable consumer goods purchased through the market.

H—Goods produced outside the market in the household sector.

S—Social sector goods and services produced and obtained outside the market.

W—Public goods and services distributed outside the market.

In practice these choices are constrained by institutional, cultural and conjunctural factors. But the range of choice configurations broadens *pari passu* with the increase in the overall productivity of the economic system and the reduction of work time required to produce the necessities of life.

The time spent on market-oriented activities generates a flow of income, whose alternative uses are consumption, investment in consumer durables, savings, or taxes. The purchase of 'durables' is in reality an investment in household producer goods rather than a consumption expenditure. Insofar as the productive capacity of the household depends, at least in part, on such previous investment, the household sector in our modern economies becomes increasingly 'colonized' by the commoditized sector.

The consumption structure is conditioned by the choices made both with respect to time and income allocation. It consists of goods and services purchased through the market, self-produced and freely distributed by the government which finances them out of taxes (see the bottom right hand side of Fig. 5.2 called the 'structure of everyday life').[14]

The type of analysis suggested here can be related to A. K. Sen's important reconceptualization of the development theory in terms of entitlements and peoples' capabilities (Sen, 1983), based on the rejection of both the utility-based welfare economics and of the fetishism of the commodity forms. It is submitted that the identification of the choice configurations in time and income allocation, relative to market/non-market options, has relevant policy implications for the mapping out of alternative entitlement bundles and for the design of policies to deal with structural unemployment. This is true not only for the Third World, but also (and perhaps even more so) for the industrialized countries. The central question for the latter is the sharing of the increases in productivity between more commodities and less work time, more equitably distributed so as to avoid the 'two-gear economy'. Fig. 5.3 indicates the range of choices when productivity goes up from T_1 to T_2: increasing the product by P_1P_2, reducing the working time by L_1L_2 while keeping the product constant, or else a combination of the two objectives. The decrease of the time spent on market-oriented activities would translate itself into

[14] This term, suggested by the title of F. Braudel's book, is used here to encompass the entire field of a generalized consumption theory.

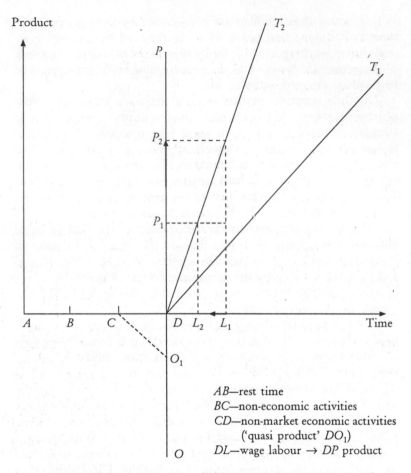

Fig. 5.3 The sharing of increased productivity

more time available for non-economic activities (BC) and/or for the non-market economic activities (CD). The whole question is to ensure to everybody a reasonable balance between the three.

An Application: Designing an Urban Eco-development Strategy[15]

The proposed planning methodology consists of five interrelated steps:

(1) An anthropological–economic analysis of the working of

[15] Based on Sachs, I. (1988b).

the 'real economy', along the lines suggested in the previous section.

(2) An ecological–economic analysis of the physical resources potential of the city: land that can be transformed into vegetable gardens allocated in priority to low-income families and senior citizens or made available for assisted self-help construction of social housing; waste and sewage that can be recycled or reused; energy and water that can be conserved at a lesser cost than the production of additional supplies; better maintenance of the stock of existing housing, infrastructure and equipment ultimately resulting in capital and resource conservation while providing additional employment.

(3) An assessment of the technologies required for the matching of human and physical resources identified in the two previous stages, exploring the whole range of the technological spectrum with special emphasis on the technologies that are at the same time not too capital-intensive.

(4) An institutional analysis of the power game and conflicts of interest among the social actors involved, of the scope for consensual or accommodating solutions rather than conflict resolution; search for new forms of partnership for development between the civil society, the State and the market forces; exploring new configurations between grassroot initiatives and local, regional and national policies.

(5) The selection of public policy instruments and packages that remove the obstacles to and are supportive of innovative urban management and peoples' resourcefulness (the ability to put to good use elements of their environments).

Citizen groups should be associated from the very outset to this search for innovative urban management, informed by the vision of a more humane and equitable city of the future, providing the necessities of life to all its inhabitants and, at the same time, unfolding manifold opportunities for interpersonal contacts, creative uses of time and a joyful life. Only in this way, it will be possible to devise and then implement concrete projects directed at specific needs of different categories of citizens—the children, the teenagers, the elderly, the women, the ethnic minorities, the disabled, etc. and based on self-help, mutual-aid, lay and volunteer care alongside with the involvement of socially concerned professionals and advocacy planners, as well as of the public services.

Education in its broadest meaning—formal and informal—is the single most important lever for raising social awareness about 'another development'—endogenous, self-reliant, need-oriented, in harmony with nature and open to institutional change (see 'What Now?', 1975). Development is a societal learning process by which people acquire positive values such as individual and collective self-reliance, the ability to effectively appropriate all their democratic rights and to make accountable to them the elected bodies and public organizations, while overcoming attitudes marked by egoism, parochialism and professional arrogance.

Deconstructing the Informal Sector: Policy Options

The challenge, as mentioned at the very beginning of this paper, is daunting. Between 1996 and the end of the century 228 million new jobs are required for those entering the labour market. By 2025, a further 870 million new jobs will be required.[16] These estimates leave intact the backlog of unattended unemployment, and underemployment.

The word 'job' is used as *pars pro toto*, insofar as it encompasses all possible forms of obtaining livelihood as wage earners, independent producers of marketable goods and services, self-provisioning of subsistence within rural and urban households or a combination of all these involving all the members of a family or extended family, adults and children.

The household is a category better suited to analyse economic strategies than individual careers chosen as the basis for statistical reporting as one more tribute to methodological individualism. The path to development leads us beyond markets and jobs to manifold forms of individual and collective realization of the fundamental human right to search for convenient means of subsistence (livelihood[17]), a basic component of the right to development.

[16] Estimates quoted by Samir Radwan, Director, Development Policies Department, ILO at the Istanbul Dialogue (ILO, 1997).
[17] This word initially used by Karl Polanyi and recently popularized by Robert Chambers has now entered the UNDP vocabulary.

Putting Mainstream Economics Upside Down

Full employment and equitable income distribution should become explicit objectives of macro-economic policies and serve as the entrypoint to the iterative procedure of designing a triple-win socially-responsive and environmentally sound growth strategy, the only one to generate meaningful development.

Table 5.1
Types of Growth According to Their Economic,
Social and Environmental Impacts[18]

	Economic	Social	Environmental
1. Savage	+	–	–
2. Socially benign	+	+	–
3. Environmentally sustainable	+	–	+
4. Triple-win (development)	+	+	+

But in market-led profit-driven growth, employment generation and income distribution are treated as residual, while environmental constraints are often bypassed. Yet, the crux of the problem was correctly grasped by the Indian economist J. C. Kumarappa in a speech on Gandhian economy delivered in 1945:

Our problem is to give employment to 400 millions of people in such a way that everyone would get his own primary needs satisfied. That means, our method of work has to be such which will distribute wealth in the process of producing wealth. Distribution and production if they do not go together or take place simultaneously, often lead to accumulation of wealth of the one side, and poverty and misery on the other.... The wealth of our country cannot be measured by the number of millionaires the country possesses. The country's well being is dependent on the happiness of the largest number of people, which means on the capacity of the largest number to satisfy their primary needs. In our country, therefore, it is not the accumulation of wealth, but the distribution of wealth as evenly as possible, that is to be desired (Kumarappa, 1945, pp. 4–5).

Lately another Indian scholar, Arun Ghosh (1996), proposed an alternative development paradigm, inspired by the theories of

[18] For more details see Chapter 1.

the great Polish economist M. Kalecki, in which an equitable distribution of national income is seen as a precondition, and not as a fallout of development. At the same time he insists on the potential for decentralized community level mobilization of unemployed or idle labour for capital formation, a remake of the Chinese experience in a democratic setup.[19]

Thus, giving up the mirage of trickle down and putting upside down mainstream economic theory, growth ought to be redirected and, whenever possible, speeded up, so long as higher rates of growth are not achieved at the expenses of employment, of equity in income distribution and of environmental prudence.

To move in this direction, fiscal reform may be necessary in order to tax capital, resources (in particular fossil energy[20]) and financial speculation (e.g. through the Tobin tax) instead of imposing prohibitive social overheads on wages and heavy VAT on services. Further progress might be achieved by better exploring non-investment sources of growth (as suggested by Kalecki): reducing the rate of real depreciation of the existing stock of productive capital, equipment, infrastructures and buildings through better maintenance on the one hand and, and on the other, increasing the rate of effective utilization of the existing productive capacities by means of better organization of the production processes and higher resource productivity.

The latter may be economically as important as labour productivity. Furthermore, it commends itself for ecological and environmental reasons insofar as it reduces the material throughput by means of energy, water and resource conservation, waste recycling

---

[19] For a discussion of this book, see Kurien, C. T. (1997). Kalecki himself (with whom I had the privilege of working from 1960 to 1968) held the view that labour-intensive investment should be encouraged and employment expanded subject only to the barrier of availability of wage goods, mainly food. That is why he was so adamant about land reforms.

[20] The Scandinavian countries and the Netherlands show the way by taxing emissions of urban dioxide. Even *The Economist* programmatically opposed to public intervention has a favourable opinion on green taxes: 'So are green taxes a good thing? Yes: they signal to polluters that the environment is valuable, and a tax system that includes them will distort economic activity less than one that does not. But governments should not need greenery as an excuse to make labour taxes less damaging. Like environmental protection, that is worthwhile anyway.'

and more extended product lifecycles.[21] Many activities resulting in higher resource productivity are fairly labour-intensive, an additional reason to consider them carefully.

Let us finally note that side by side with macroeconomic reforms and policies performed at the national level, which still largely determine the level of employment and labour regimes (Lee, E., 1997), there is considerable room for improving the international environment, which is fairly negative for the developing countries at present as a consequence of the globalization processes. Nordic countries and the Netherlands are the only ones to honour the commitment to spend 0.7 per cent of their GDP on official development assistance, which has shrunk to 0.25 per cent of the joint GDP of industrialized member-countries of OECD. These are very small figures indeed, compared to the outflow of capital from the South to North on account of debt service (420 billion dollars between 1980 and 1992), royalties, dividends, repatriated profits, underpaid raw materials and overpaid imports, international trade conditions being far from equitable. As Pierre Schori, Sweden's Minister for International Development Cooperation, put it in a lecture celebrating the 50th anniversary of the Marshall Plan, 'the spectre of a global apartheid is emerging. A nightmare where the rich of the rich, and the rich of the poor entrench themselves in fortified and mental ghettos' (Schori, F., 1996, p. 10). His call for a New Deal for Internationalism fell on deaf ears in Washington judging by the American policy towards the UN system and the failure of the Rio plus five recent Summit. However, further consideration of this question goes beyond the scope of this paper.[22]

To conclude this section on macroeconomic reforms and policies, if regular jobs are created through triple-win strategies in significant numbers, the volume of informal (non-criminal) activities is likely to decrease, triggering out the easing of the

[21] See on this subject the already quoted book by von Weizsäcker, Lovins and Lovins, (1997). The authors propose doubling of world output with halving of inputs.

[22] For a cogent catalogue of the demands of the South see the presentation by Martin Khor, Director, Third World Network on 'Trade, Environment and Sustainable Development' on 15 April 1997 in New York at the fifth session of The Commission on Sustainable Development, United Nations.

downward pressure of the reserve army of unemployed and underemployed on the wage rates.

But even under the most optimistic assumptions about the political willingness and the capacity of governments to go ahead into reforms that will put their economies on the virtuous path of socially equitable and ecologically sustainable growth, it would be unrealistic to expect, for many years to come, the absorption of all informal activities by the organized sector along the lines of naïve dualistic models (in vogue during the fifties and sixties) figuring out the progressive siphoning out by the 'modern sector' of surplus labour reserve parked in the 'traditional sector'. The more so that we are going through an employment displacing phase of technical progress worldwide both in the processing and tertiary activities.[23] It would be even more unrealistic to expect the Third World countries to establish a comprehensive safety net for the unemployed along the lines of European welfare states. The pale copies established by populist governments in Latin America at best benefit a tiny workers' aristocracy.

This is not to say, however, that we should accept as a fatality the 'two-gear model', based on the polarization between the minority of the happy who are included in the thriving modern globalized economy, and those who are excluded from it and condemned to squeeze out their meagre livelihood from informal activities in an unfulfilling life of daily struggle for survival, of squalor and of exclusion, compounded by all sorts of direct and indirect exploitation. Much can and ought to be done to improve their wretched condition *hic et nunc* through sectoral strategies addressing different components of the deconstructed 'informal sector' (more exactly the spectrum of non-criminal informal activities). The remainder of this paper is devoted to this subject.

Family Agriculture and Rural Development: One Billion Job Equivalents in Ten Years?

Contrary to an entrenched prejudice, properly modernized family agriculture and rural development still offers an important, ecologically sustainable development alternative. Instead of encouraging

---

[23] As much as one-third of all jobs were suppressed in the Brazilian manufacturing industries during the last decade. Downsizing has also significantly affected the banking sector.

accelerated urbanization, we ought to put on the agenda the search for more balanced rural–urban configurations (Sachs, I., ed., 1996a). The mimetic reproduction on a worldwide scale of the historical path followed by the industrialized countries, which succeeded in emptying their villages in a few decades,[24] seems hardly possible on the account of very high costs of urbanization and is undesirable, judging by the Latin American experience. Rapid deruralization prompted by an ill adapted model of labour-displacing agricultural modernization (the 'pull factor') and the mirage of good urban life contrasting with the rural hopelessness (the 'push factor') led to an explosion of shantytowns, sort of 'pre-cities' or purgatories, in which the refugees from the countryside await their turn for effective urbanization, meaning by this a decent job, affordable housing and effective appropriation of all human rights—political, civic, civil social, economic and cultural (see Sachs, I. and R. Abramovay, 1996b). Some of the largest megacities sprung all over the Third World in the last half-century, to become environmental nightmares and foci of uncontrolled violence. Both these evils affect mostly the poor population of suburbs and shanties, as the rich wall themselves in self-imposed affluent ghettos (see Pires Caldeira, T., 1997).

The push factor is very strong indeed. Cities are attractive because, paraphrasing Jules Michelet, they act as big 'lotteries of life', offering many opportunities, if not to the first generation migrant, to his children or grandchildren, in contrast with the hopeless deadlock prevailing in villages bypassed by economic and social progress. However, there are relatively few winning tickets compared to the swelling numbers of gamblers trying their chance. Moreover, the opportunity cost of urbanization of the 'pre-city' dwellers is very high compared to the modest outlays required to modernize the already existing family operated small landholdings, to transform millions of landless agricultural labourers into prosperous peasants by carrying land reforms in countries endowed with favourable land–man ratio, while, at the same time, 'urbanizing the countryside' by extending to rural areas the non-existent or blatantly deficient health, educational and cultural services.

[24] Mass migrations of European peasants to America played a significant role in this process, worth remembering in the context of present discussions on globalization. The marketizers are all for the free circulation of capital and goods, but not so for the movement of labour.

Albeit for different reasons, looking for alternative rural development strategies is as much a priority for densely populated and land scarce poor countries like India and China, as for those Latin American and African countries which still have huge reserves of uncultivated land and low rural population densities.

For the latter, an excessively rapid urbanization means a diversion of funds that could be used more effectively to meet the basic needs of their populations, a foregone historical opportunity to take advantage of their natural resources endowment with a view to achieving a more balanced rural–urban configuration and a more equitable society.

As for the former, were the two Asian giants to follow the Latin-American pace of urbanization, the sheer magnitude of the absolute numbers of people potentially involved in rural–urban migrations would jeopardize their development prospect by diverting to urban construction a far too large proportion of their investment capacity, notwithstanding notoriously high savings ratios.

In a report which did not attract the attention it deserved, the independent International Commission on Peace and Food chaired by M. S. Swaminathan (1994) argued, extrapolating the 'Prosperity 2000 Strategy for India', that the goal of one billion jobs in ten years was achievable through a low cost strategy by using agriculture as an engine of growth.[25]

The figure is surprisingly high, as are the 100 million jobs proposed in the Indian context. But instead of speculating how many additional years will be required to reach this target, let us concentrate on the logic underlying this proposal. It seeks to tap the competitive advantage of small-scale family farms in labour-intensive agricultural crops and allied industries. About half of new jobs (45 million) will be generated on farms by raising productivity through imposed management of micro-nutrients and water, expanding the total irrigated area, emphasizing on more labour-intensive commercial crops such as sugar, cotton, fruit, flowers and vegetables, sericulture, inland and coastal aquaculture, reclamation of wasteland for forestry and fodder and increasing subsidiary

---

[25] By comparison tourism and travel, the sector of the economy which claims the first rank with respect to employment generation expects to add world-wide some 130 million jobs in ten years to the 255 million existing at present (*Le Monde*, 8 July 1997).

incomes from animal husbandry and poultry. The additional agricultural production will produce raw materials for expansion of agro-industries and generate non-farm 10 million rural jobs. The multiplier effect of increased rural incomes will furthermore create another 45 million rural and urban jobs in industry and services.

It is claimed that the average cost per additional job in India will be less than 1000 dollars, roughly one-tenth the average cost of jobs in India's private sector.[26] Funding will come from a mix of public and private investment with the government playing a central role as catalyst, enabler and pioneer rather than owner or manager.

The neuralgic point in this plan is its heavy reliance on agricultural exports predicated on the opening of markets in industrial countries, a legitimate, albeit politically unrealistic, demand on the part of Third World countries. In spite of their free-trade rhetoric, neither the European Union nor the United States are prepared to give up their protectionist agricultural policies.

By contrast, it is not clear whether the Swaminathan report fully appreciated the potential of using surplus food to launch large-scale programmes of public works and housing construction.

In the long run, non-food biomass production for energy and industrial purposes is bound to greatly increase its share in total

[26] This is a very low figure indeed. A draft report commissioned by the Brazilian Minister for Land Tenure Affairs (MEPF/INCRA, June 1997) estimates in 15.9 billion reais (approximately 15 billion dollars) the front payments required to settle through land reform till the year 2002 one million landless families. A significant part of this sum will be recovered as it will be advanced in form of loans. Moreover, payments for expropriated land will be made in negotiated bonds, not in cash. The authors of the report assume three direct job equivalents per family and 'at least twice as many indirect jobs' (apparently a heroic assumption). They do not include in their financial estimate the additional investment required by these jobs induced through the multiplier effect. On the other hand, they apparently did not consider the value of non-monetary investment carried out by settlers and their families. At any rate, 5000 dollars per job equivalent (plus the induced employment with unspecified additional costs) compare very favourably with the average investment required to generate a job in the industrial sector. According to data circulated by the Brazilian press in the motor-car industry (an extreme case), it may range from 250 to 750 thousand dollars (with 3 to 7 indirect jobs generated for each direct job with unspecified additional investment).

agri- and silvicultural output. M. S. Swaminathan has extensively written that the prospect for a modern biomass-based civilization is not only possible but also necessary if we are serious about ecological sustainability. Tropical countries ought to seize the comparative advantage of their climates, long held as a handicap, and engage into leap-frogging in the realm of biotechnologies capable of increasing the biomass yields at the one end of the production chain while opening up the range of biomass-derived products at the other end. The Brazilian sociologist Gilberto Freyre pioneered almost forty years ago the idea of an original modern civilization of the tropics and founded to this effect in Recife a Seminar of Tropicology. His intuition was basically correct, even though his own views on 'lusotropicalism' arose deserved criticism.[27]

Let us finally add that whenever a ton of petrol is substituted by ethanol or vegetable oils, a backward linkage employment multiplier is set in motion and the pressure is reinforced for a careful management of life-support systems—climate, soils, water, forest—on which the production of biomass depends.

Regularizing the Illegal City

The majority of Third World urbanites live in illegally built and owned houses, purchased or rented in booming informal real estate markets or else self-constructed, often on illegally occupied land, through family effort and neighbours' help (mutual aid), with materials partly purchased, partly collected on the garbage dumps with occasional intervention of professional craftsmen more often than not working informally.

On the eve of the Vancouver Habitat Conference, John Turner (1976) pioneered the analysis of people's extraordinary display of ingeniosity, entrepreneurship, years long patient efforts and financial acrobacy to finally succeed in housing themselves.[28] It is nowadays commonly accepted that these efforts should be encouraged and assisted, in sharp contrast with earlier attempts at repressing the self-help construction under the pretext of its illegality and sending bulldozers and police to erase shantytowns

---

[27] See on this point Chapter 3 in this volume.

[28] His book, based on earlier articles, had as title *Housing by People* and contained a chapter on 'housing as a verb'!

(those dangerous cancers on the body of the beautiful city) and relocate their inhabitants in distant suburbs, far removed from the upper-class sections of the town but also from their working places.

The 'illegal city' is there to stay. Therefore urban programmes are being redirected at improving the rehabilitation of slums and of peripheric settlements, and the extension to them of basic services.

By changing unrealistic laws regulating urban property and too strict building codes, large segments of hitherto illegal city may be legalized overnight. In a market society, the benefits of such an operation for its inhabitants are substantial. To legally own a house—even a very modest one—is a first step to effective citizenhood, the possibility to knock at the door of a bank instead of the moneylender, to pay less for electrical power and water by bypassing the intermediaries.

This segment of urban reform is relatively easy to implement. Yet, it leaves unsolved a far larger problem! How to house the homeless, and relocate those who live in primitive shacks, not to speak of the millions of refugees from the countryside still to come. In Brazil alone substandard housing affects 12 million families out of a total of 37.8 million, including a deficit of 3.4 million dwellings, as against an annual average of 50 thousand dwellings for low-income families built over the last 30 years through public housing programmes (O Estado de São Paulo, 31 May 1997).[29]

How to reconcile decent habitational standards with affordability resembles the squaring of the circle. Subsidizing (or cross subsidizing by putting to contribution the middle and upper-class buyers of houses) is certainly necessary. But even so, the experience of most developing and former socialist countries shows that large-scale industrialized housing construction programmes fail in delivering the number of dwellings corresponding to the demand, either because of the high cost involved in such programmes or of organizational problems. Apparently, solutions are to be searched in new partnerships between the interested families, the public

[29] For an up-to-date description of the urban conditions in the world, see Satterwhaite, D. (1996) and for the analysis of the Brazilian experience in popular public housing policies, Sachs–Jeantet, C. (1990).

authorities, the market and the 'third sector'—the non-profit citizens organizations, cooperatives and mutual-aid institutions, 'all that is private yet public' (Rubem Cesar Fernandes). The future belongs to assisted self-help construction made possible through the interaction of the non-market, the market and the public sector.

Overcoming Informality through Public–Private Partnerships: The Pivotal Role of the 'Third Sector'

Housing is a major but by no means a unique sphere of informal activities which are conspicuously present in trade, transportation, services, petty industrial and artisanal production, not to speak of healers, fortune tellers, priests and moneylenders and of a web of traditional—religious, mutual-aid and even financial institutions, such as the *tontines*, sort of African mutual-aid funds.[30]

The word informal suggests that formality is the rule and informality the exception. In many Third World cities the opposite is true. de Soto was right in denouncing formality in Peru as an expensive luxury. In the African context, ENDA (a Daker based NGO) has come in defence of a genuine, yet fragile popular economy embedded in local culture, customs and consumption patterns. In the absence of public social safety nets, it offers the only chance of survival to all those who, for good or bad reasons, left behind their native villages.

Opinions differ widely about the attitude to adopt informal activities. Some academic economists choose to ignore their very existence as they do not fit their models of stylized market economy (*tant pis pour la réalité*). Others consider (even if they do not say it publicly) that informal activities are doomed to disappear, as they constitute an obstacle to the expansion of the modern market economy. Insofar as informal activities do not respect legal, social, health and quality standards and furthermore evade taxes, they violate the rules of fair competition. In the same way,

[30] A good instance of complex interrelations between religious institutions and economy is provided by the way in which the Mouvide brotherhood is implicit in the functioning of the Senegalese economy, specially in the Tonta duty-free city, described by *Newsweek* as 'the hub of Senegal's transportation and real-estate empires, the booming informal sector and the peanut trade, the nation's main source of foreign exchange'. The Mouvide blend of religion and business is also present in the informal activities of the Senegalese community in New York.

traditional practitioners should not be allowed to exercise professions reserved for holders of legally recognized diplomas.

At the other end of the spectrum, the unconditional hypocritical defenders of the informal economy present it as a safety-valve, an efficient and marvellously cheap substitute for the social safety nets and an excuse for discharging the State from the obligation of acting to protect the poor and the excluded.

A less cynical stance consists in recommending marginal actions in favour of the informal activities, in order to improve their resilience. Extending small credits to street food vendors or *marchandes de quatre saisons* through Grameen-type banks (of Bangladesh) may help the poor to resist the competition of Mc Donalds type fast-food chains and supermarkets and squeeze a meagre living from their traditional activities. This survival expedient is better than outright starving. The dissemination of Grameen banks and similar institutions is by all means commendable, the more so that they are based on an imaginative concept of collective responsibility, which triggers a learning process of collective community action.

But this kind of limited initiatives makes only sense as part of a much broader development package. To see in Grameen banks a 'Copernican revolution in development financing' hinted at by some World Bank officials is simply preposterous. Meaningful development strategies require the mobilization of funds of a totally different magnitude and the synergic action of meso-level policies going beyond the mere support of traditional informal activities. The latter ought to be upgraded, transformed and progressively included in the formal economy through development strategies implemented by a variety of public–private partnerships, in which the 'third sector'[31] could play a pivotal role.

The operators of informal activities need by and large the same kind of support as family farmers:

- preferential access to knowledge and modern skills through education and technical extension services;[32]

[31] Let us recall that this category encompasses institutions engaged in market-oriented activities on a non-profit basis (e.g. cooperatives) and the 'voluntary sector' which is 'neither public, neither market' in Robert Kuttner's words (1977, p. 351).

[32] With special emphasis on skilled labour-intensive technologies building on centuries-old traditions of craftsmanship.

– provision of cheap credit;
– marketing facilities for their services and goods, including the possibility of provisioning public institutions (schools, offices, hospitals, cantonments and prisons).

Their workshops and factories will gain in efficiency by being pooled together in industrial estates and technological parks, where they can get technical, organizational and marketing assistance.[33]

A simplified legal, fiscal and book-keeping status for micro-enterprises will help their inclusion into the regular economy.

Production of care in the society constitutes another area particularly suited for a synergic action of all the four categories of actors– informal, public, private and 'third sector'. Family and kinship solidarity networks are a valuable asset. At the same time, the state responsibilities should be clearly reaffirmed. Moral criteria must take precedence over hard economics.[34] The more so in Third World countries where considerable opportunities exist for creating a large number of jobs in these fields with quite limited investment.

Wages and salaries paid to teachers, paramedical staff and social workers in Third World countries are much lower than the wages and salaries of their counterparts in the industrialized countries, yet their 'productivity' is much the same. The Third World countries thus have a considerable comparative advantage over the industrialized countries as regards the production costs of social services, provided that resources are not squandered on the construction of luxury schools or hospitals. The catalytic use of

---

[33] There are many lessons to draw from the extremely successful post-War decentralized industrialization of the Northeastern Italy, the so-called 'terza Italia', although it does not offer an easily transposable model.

[34] This point has been forcefully made by the former Director-General of WHO, H. T. Mahler: If you judge success on the basis of hard economics alone, well—kill off the elderly, kill off the weak, kill off the disabled! Get rid of social pathology by eliminating its victims! Do you think that is idle rhetoric? Has it not happened in the course of this century? Surely recent history should drive home to us the need to temper economic values with social values, with human values, with compassion for the plight of the health have nots. Should chaotic economic indicators be allowed to dictate human affairs, or should human goals dictate them?' (H. T. Mahler, address to the 40th World Health Assembly, 8 May 1987).

modern technologies should make it possible to develop systems for providing social services that not only create many new jobs, but are also efficient.

Third World countries would be, therefore, well advised to reverse the sequence of events followed by the industrialized countries. They can and should begin the construction of welfare states adapted to their circumstances without waiting to become rich (see Sachs, 1971). Instead of reducing social expenditure as part of the austerity imposed by adjustment programmes, they should increase the relative share of resources allocated to the social sector. Even a small marginal change of this kind would bring about a considerable improvement in the quality of life. In the same way, aid from the industrialized countries, to the extent to which it exists, should take the form of grants (not of loans) for the development of social services and the creation of jobs in these sectors.

Applying intersectoral approaches to the pursuit of social goals enlarges the scope for a great variety of partnerships in different realms, as shown by the example of health (see Fig. 5.4).

More generally, as persuasively argued by Paul Streeten (op. cit. p. 68):

It is not at all clear that our society cannot use plenty of health-workers, nurses, child rearers, gardeners, plumbers, sweepers, protectors and re-storers of the environment, and other service-workers who do not need the high and scarce skills demanded by modern technology and whose services cannot be replaced by either computers or imported low-cost goods from low-income countries (though imported low-cost workers should be welcomed). Many of these jobs are, however, in the currently despised or neglected public sector and may call for even more despised higher taxation. They are also often ill-paid and not recognized as valuable. We need to change our valuation of such work and should guarantee minimum standards of reward for them.

Two comments are in order here. A need-oriented logic is called for as the entry-point into development planning, which is not tantamount to underestimating the difficulty in transforming needs into at least partly market-solvable demand and/or finding ways of financing their satisfaction. On the other hand, the challenge for innovative solutions lies more in the realm of social engineering than in the one-sided pursuit of technical progress.

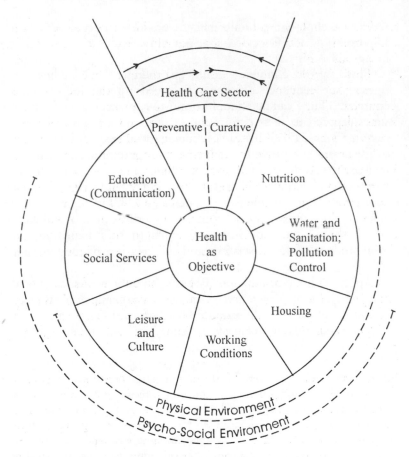

Fig. 5.4 Multisectoral approach to health

Concluding Remarks

In all these endeavours, the 'third sector' is well placed to act as go-between informal operators, the public sector and the regular markets.

However, in order to successfully reorient development strategies along these lines three conditions must be fulfilled:

(1) The 'third sector' should be consolidated and expanded with an efficient cooperative system as its backbone. References can be made here to the historical experience of Scandinavian

countries: rural cooperatives coupled with popular education played a decisive role in their development.[35]

* Non-profit institutions and charities resorting partly to voluntary labour and mobilizing private funds for socially-oriented projects of course have their place in the 'third sector', but the indigenization of NGOs is badly needed. Too often they depend almost exclusively on external funding and end up interiorizing foreign concerns instead of identifying genuine local priorities.[36]

By contrast, a much greater attention should be given to customary forms of resource management, the variegated traditions of mutual-aid and diverse local solidarity networks. These should be used as a foundation for genuine decentralization and people's effective empowerment (see on this point Friedmann, J., 1992).

(2) The 'third sector' should be instrumental in exploring the potential for mobilizing latent human and physical resources for local development projects, initiated and identified at the grassroots level through popular consultation and implemented by means of a contract between all the actors involved, pooling public and private financial resources with non-monetary investment (through voluntary labour of the interested populations). An experience of this kind has been attempted on an unprecedented scale in the Indian state of Kerala on the basis of revitalized 'panchayats' (local councils).[37] Its success will put back on the international agenda the somewhat discredited idea of strategic planning, based on a negotiation among all the social actors and their entering into contractual arrangements—a sort of enlarged and generalized tripartism.

(3) The State should be prepared to, and equipped for, assuring the demanding task of democratically guiding the developmental process reconceptualized as 'expansion of positive freedoms' (A. K. Sen) more specifically of regulating the working of 'negotiated economies' with a view to promoting synergies between its various public and private components. Robert Kuttner's (1977)

---

[35] For an interesting comparison of Denmark with Uruguay, see Senghaas, D. (1985).

[36] This seems particularly true of the NGOs acting in the environmental field.

penetrating study of the virtues and limits of markets and spirited defence of 'mixed economies' offers a convincing plea for a balance between market, State and civil society. *Everything is not for sale.* If people are to join in collective endeavours outside the market's logic of private purchasing power and private profit maximization, markets must be kept in their place and properly regulated by a strong state. This calls in turn for a *strong* consensual and deliberative democracy as a foundational value choice, in order to prevent the State to be its own source of tyranny (p. 344).

This may be a tall order in our age of market celebration, government denigration, degraded politics and ruthless globalization. This is one more reason to give the topmost priority to the reform of the State, freeing it from the pathologies of excessive statism and patrimonialism, while rejecting at the same time the mirage of minimum State and laissez-faire advocated by the neoliberal extremists. The World Bank itself dedicated its *1997 Development Report* to this crucial question of the role of the State. Is it too optimistic to assume that the neoliberal counter-revolution is receding?

References

Archambault, E. and Greffe, X. (eds) (1984), *Les économies non officielles*, Ed. La Découverte, Paris.

de Soto, Hernan (1986), *El Otro Sendero*, Lima.

Friedmann, J. (1992), *Empowerment: The Politics of Alternative Development*, Blackwell, Oxford.

Ghosh, A. (1996), *Paradigms of Economic Development*, Indian Institute of Advanced Study, Shimla.

[37] Three million people—one-tenth of the total population of Kerala—took part in local meetings and by participating in data collection and preparation of 'Development Reports' by the 990 panchayats, 51 municipalities and 3 city corporations of the State. Kerala thus became the first Indian State to have basic data banks at the local level. The campaign also identified nearly 30,000 technically competent persons outside the government system at the village and panchayat ward levels who could contribute to the local development. Kerala is in reality trying out a system of planning for development at different levels from the village to the state level (see the correspondence on 'Planning from Below' by R. Krishna Kumar in the Indian magazine *Frontline* dated 7 March 1997).

IBASE/SEBRAE (1997), 'Informalidade—Cidadania—Empreendimentos Informais in Rio de Janeiro', Rio De Janeiro.

ILO, (1972), *Employment, Income and Equity. A Strategy for Increasing Productive Employment in Kenya*, Geneva.

—— (1997), 'The Future of Urban Employment' (5th June 1996, Istanbul, Turkey), Report and Proceedings, Habitat II Dialogue for the 21st Century.

Kumarappa, J. C. (1945), *The Gandhian Economy and Other Essays*, Maganvadi, Waralia.

Kurien, C. T. (1997), 'Development with Equity', *Economic and Political Weekly*, May 10.

Kuttner, R. (1997), *Everything for Sale, the Virtues and Limits of Markets*, Alfred A. Knopf, NewYork.

Lautier, B., (1994), *L'économie informelle dans le Tiers Monde*, Ed. La Découverte, Paris.

Lee, E. (1997), 'La mondialisation et l'emploi: des craintes justifiées?' *Revue Internationale du Travail*, n° 5, 1996 and *Problèmes Economiques*, n° 2517, 23 April.

MEPF/INCRA (1997), *Programa de Reforma Agrária e Desenvolvimento Sustantável* (versão preliminar), Brasilia.

Pietila, H. (1997), 'The triangle of the human economy: household-cultivation-industrial production. An attempt at making visible the human economy in toto', *Ecological Economics* 20, pp. 113–27.

Pires Caldeira, T. (1997), *The City of Walls*, California University Press, (in press).

Portes, A. (1994), 'The Informal Economy and Its Paradoxes', in Smelser, N. J. and Swedberg, R. (eds), *The Handbook of Economic Sociology*, Princeton University Press, Princeton, pp. 426–49.

Sachs, I. (1971), 'A Welfare State for Poor Countries', *Economic and Political Weekly*, vol. VI, no. 3–4, pp. 367–70.

—— (1987), *Development and Planning*, Cambridge University Press, Cambridge, New York and New Rochelle, Paris, Ed. de la Maison des Sciences de l'Homme, p. 134.

—— (1988a), 'Market, Non-Market, Quasi-Market and the "Real" Economy', Arrow, Kenneth J. (ed.), *The Balance between Industry and Agriculture in Economic Development, vol. 1, Basic Issues*, Proceedings of the Eighth World Congress of the International Economic Association, Delhi, Macmillan Press, pp. 218–31.

—— (1988b), 'Work, food and energy in urban eco-development', *Economic and Political Weekly*, Bombay, vol. XIII, no. 9, 27 February, pp. 425–44.

———— (ed.) (1996a), *Quelles Villes, pour quel développement?*, Presses Universitaires de France/Nouvelle Encyclopédie Diderot, Paris.

Sachs, I. and Abramovay, R. (1996b), 'Nouvelles configurations villes-campagnes', in *Land and Rural/Urban Linkages in The Twenty-First Century*, Proceedings of the Second United Nations Conference on Human Settlements (Habitat II-Dialogue 6), Istanbul, June.

Sachs-Jeantet, Céline (1990), *São Paulo, politiques publiques et habitat populaire*, Editions MSH, Paris.

Satterwhaite, D. (ed.) (1996), *Global Report on Human Settlements*, UNCHS/Oxford University Press, Oxford and New York.

Schori, F. (1996), 'From Marshall to Post-Communism' (First Lecture of the Marshall Plan 50th Anniversary Distinguished Lecture Series at Smithsonian Institution), Washington.

Sen, A. K. (1983), 'Goods and People', in Urquidi, V. L. (ed.), *Structural Change, Economic Interdependence and World Development, vol. 1 Basic Issues*, London, Macmillan, 1987, pp. 153–78.

Senghaas, D. (1985), *The European Experience*, Zed Books, London.

Streeten, P. (1997), 'Some Reflections on Social Exclusion in Social Exclusion and Anti-Poverty Policy: A Debate' in Gore, Ch. and Figueiredo, J. B. (eds), International Institute for Labour Studies/UNDP, New York–Geneva, pp. 66–73.

Swaminathan, M. S., et al. (1994), *Uncommon Opportunities—An Agenda for Peace and Equitable Development*, Report of the International Commission on Peace and Food, Zed Books, London and New Jersey.

Thurow, Leslie (1995), foreword to Schafer, T. and Faux, J., *Reclaiming Prosperity: A Blueprint for Progressive Economic Reform*, Economic Policy Institute, Washington.

Turner, J. (1976), *Housing by People* (French translation: *Le logement est votre affaire*, 1979, Seuil, Paris).

United Nations (1996), *Informal Sector Development in Africa*, New York.

von Weizsäcker, E., Lovins, A. B. and Lovins, L. H. (1997), *Factor Four, Doubling Wealth—Halving Resource-Use*, The New Report to the Club of Rome, Earthscan Publications Ltd, London.

'What Now?', (1975), Dag Hammarskjöld Report on Development and International Cooperation, *Development Dialogue*, n° 1/2, Uppsala.

Rethinking Development Strategies in the Aftermath of the Asian Crisis

Ideas matter insofar as they inform the action taken by politicians. In a thought provoking book entitled *Turning Point*, Robert Ayres (1998) argues that the present growth paradigm will prove increasingly unsustainable. He may be right but the change will not be made overnight. Yet, to the future historians of economic thought, 1998 may appear as a turning point for another reason. The crisis unleashed by the collapse of the Thai currency in July 1997 shattered the undisputed domination of the neoliberal gospel in government circles and international organizations, given the inadequacy of the solutions proposed by IMF and their catastrophic social consequences. With some optimism, we may even expect that the twenty-year neoliberal interlude is nearing its end.

The Chief Economist of the World Bank has been lecturing around the world about the need to move towards the post-Washington consensus (Stiglitz, J. E, 1998). The IMF came under severe criticism from unexpected sources (Paul Krugmann, 1998; Jeffrey Sachs, 1998; Henry Kissinger, 1998). Foreign exchange controls regained their respectability in the eyes of several mainstream economists and Jagdish Bhagwati himself (1998) denounced the excessive liberalization of capital movements. Peter Drucker (1998) pointed out the one-dimensionality of capitalism as a system because it idolizes economics as the be all and end all of life.[1] John Gray went a step further considering that a democratic free market capitalism is an utopia, as

democracy and free market are rivals and not allies.... In a democracy, the rights of citizens are guaranteed. But free market just deprives them from these rights. Everything is subordinated to free competition, leaving helpless those who are less fit to compete and, therefore, need most to be protected (Gray, 1998).[2]

Several critics of the IMF packages decided to revisit Keynesianism, as a more appropriate economic doctrine, to deal with a real economy. This is certainly a welcome shift, provided one makes a distinction between conservative and progressive versions of Keynesianism.

It is my belief that we ought to go back to the writings of Michal Kalecki and Joan Robinson, to the extent to which they emphasize the centrality of employment (and/or self-employment) and of the primary income distribution associated with it, distinct from redistribution *ex post*. While challenging the straightjacket of orthodox monetary policies, which is not tantamount to advocate excessive deficit financing, we also ought to put the active role of the State in the steering of mixed economies and their democratic regulation, back on the agenda.[3]

---

[1] To him, 'whole dimensions of what it means to be a human being and treated as one are not incorporated into the economic calculus of capitalism. For such a myopic system to dominate other aspects of life is not good for any society'.

[2] This is all the more significant as it comes from a distinguished professor of The London School of Economics who considers himself an advocate of democratic capitalism.

[3] Quite significantly, the World Bank's 1997 Development Report had as its main topic the State in a changing world (Banque Mondiale, 1997).

In Brazil 'the need for redefining and rebuilding the state has become a question of highest priority' (Presidency of the Republic, White Paper, 1995, p. 14), even though the results up to now have been deceptive. This concern is shared by many other nations from the South and from the North alike, not speaking of the post-socialist Russia, where a void of legitimate State authority yields mafias instead of efficient laissez-faire (Kuttner, R., 1997, p. 330, see also Ziegler, J., 1998).

What are the Different Development Alternatives Available to Different States?

Torn between the ideological poles of *totalitarianism, etatism* and *dogmatic liberalism*,[4] the debate on the role of the State has occupied centre stage in development theories. Since the end of the Second World War, it has gone through three stages summarized in the following way by H. J. Chang:

the age of regulation (1945–70), when most countries saw an increase in government intervention, in the forms of increased government expenditure, nationalization, extension of regulation, with accompanying developments in interventionist economic theories;

the transition period (1970–80), when the post-War regimes of intervention began to be exposed to significant political attack, helped by the rise of anti-interventionist economic theories;

the age of deregulation (1980–the present), when many countries attempted to reduce government intervention, by privatisation, budget cuts, and deregulation, often drawing justification from the theoretical extensions of the anti-interventionist theories that originated in the 1970s and were elaborated during the 1980s (Chang, H. J., 1997a, p 724).[5]

The old models have run out of steam. 'Real socialism' collapsed essentially for political reasons. Lack of transparency and of democratic institutions allowing for an effective social control of the working of the State brought about the emergence of pathological forms of shortsighted statism, clientelism and patrimonialism with devastating effects on the efficiency of the economic system.

Under different names (privatization of the State, bureaucratic rings, crony capitalism) similar pathologies have plagued more or less authoritarian regimes in the periphery of the capitalist system, in Latin America, Africa and Asia. They even succeeded in perverting the model developmental State in South Korea. However, the crisis there was caused by lack of effective regulation and monitoring of the banking system, a default not excess of the developmental State.

[4] I borrow those terms from Mikaly Simai's preface to Chang, H. J. and R. Rowthorn (eds) (1995).

[5] See also Chang, H. J. and R. Rowthorn (eds) (1995) with two important contributions by the editors and a collection of WIDER papers on the role of the State in economic change, Deane, P. (1989) and Block, F. (1994).

The ideologues of *laissez-faire* were quick to interpret the collapse of the centrally planned economies in the Soviet bloc as a proof *a contrario* of the excellence of their model. Yet, as observed by Eric Hobsbawm (1994, pp. 563–9), this counter-utopia to the collapsed real socialism is also demonstrably bankrupt. All the miracles of the twentieth century were accomplished against *laissez-faire*, not through it.[6]

A far more disturbing question than the collapse of these two polar extremes is the disorientation of the *middle way* programmes and policies, that attempt to pragmatically mix public and private realms, market and planning, State and business and, later on, civil society.

The social-democratic paradigm, seeking efficiency through market-led growth and equity through generous redistribution schemes,[7] is also in crisis, as acknowledged by the leaders of the socialist parties.[8] It proved fairly successful from 1945 to the late seventies, while Western economies were going through a period of high post-War growth and almost full employment. But it cannot cope anymore through mere redistribution of income with the present levels of unemployment, social exclusion and growing social inequality within nations and between nations. Taxes cannot be increased above a certain limit without being fiercely resisted by capitalists afraid of loosing their competitive edge and threatening to move their businesses to countries that offer a more favourable fiscal regime.[9] In reality, wealth buys, among other things, power and power vested in private hands resists income redistribution.

[6] For a convincing argument on the entrepreneurial role played by the American State during the period of catching up in the late nineteenth century, see Kozul-Wright, R. (1995).

[7] The following sentence is attributed to a West-European socialist leader: 'Let us take good care of the capitalist cows, so as to have plenty of milk that we shall distribute to everyone'.

[8] Cf. a recent article by Dominique Strauss-Kahn (French Minister of Finance): 'Après le succès, puis l'épuisement du modèle social-démocrate issu de l'après-guerre, la pensée de gauche est une nouvelle fois à reconstruire' (Le Nouvel Observateur, 19–25 février 1998, p. 45). English translation: 'The socio-democratic model evolved after the Second World War had been successful, but then later ran out of stream; so the left must once more reconstruct its thoughts.'

[9] For a critique of competitiveness as an all-prevailing ideology, see Group of Lisbon, The (Petrella, R. et al.) (1993).

Hence, while striving to maintain safety nets for the needy, the urgent need is to address two more fundamental questions:

The *primary income distribution* inscribed in the production system and the *asset redistribution*.

The emphasis should be on the distribution of wealth in the process of producing wealth (Kumarappa, 1950). Full employment (including self-employment) and *ex-ante* defined relative shares of wages and profits in the national income should therefore become the entry points in the iterative process of designing the development strategy, instead of being treated as results of the market and profit-led growth.[10]

On the other hand, as persuasively argued by J. P. Fitoussi and P. Rosanvallon (1996), to foster equality of chances, another tenet of the social democratic paradigm, it is necessary to democratize access to such assets like housing, transportation, urban environment, side by side with education and health. This calls, however, for a sustained and greatly increased effort in public investment, something private businessmen are not prepared to accept easily in the present conjuncture. After the fall of the Berlin wall and the disintegration of the Soviet Union their stance has hardened, as if the world were pushed back to the pre-1929 period putting into brackets the Fordist pact and the Keynesian consensus.

Under the present circumstances it will not be easy to evolve new *middle way democratic regimes*, which, without loosing their economic efficiency, strike the right balance between public and private, market and planning, short-term contingencies and long-term visions informed by the ideals of social justice and harmony with nature.

None of the actually existing varieties of capitalism[11] has up to now succeeded in this endeavour, standing up to the challenge of the crisis which has undermined the effectiveness of the three main areas of action in the contemporary world: the State, the market and science and technology (Banuri, T., 1998).

---

[10] In other words the conventional economics must be put upside down, in consonance with the views of the great Polish economist Michal Kalecki, See on this point Kurien, C. T. (1997).

[11] See on this point M. Albert (1990), Crouch, C. and Streeck, W. (eds) (1996), Todd, E. (1998), and for an overview of the emergence and, lately on, of the onslaught against the Welfare State, Bairoch, P. (1997) (pp. 446–545).

The State has lost part of its autonomy of action on account of the globalization processes, even though the paralyzing effects of the globalization are often overstated.[12] More serious has been the weakening of the post-War 'Keynesian consensus' over the legitimacy of State intervention under the combined impact of neo-classical critiques of government failures (justified up to a point by the excesses and pathologies of 'statism'), the liberal critique of human rights violations by many governments, the emergence of the civil society and the collapse of Soviet-type centralized and comprehensive planning. For the free-marketers, politics and government are evil because of the allegedly negative impact on the allocative efficiency of the markets.

At the same time, the market did not live up to the promise of growth and social uplift that were supposed to come through liberalization. Presented as a solution, liberalization appears to be much more part of the problem[13] in the light of the dismal performance of the world economy in the eighties and nineties. A quote from the 1997 UNCTAD's Report is in order here:

The big story of the world economy since the early 1980s has been the unleashing of market forces. The deregulation of domestic markets and their opening up to international competition have become universal features. The 'invisible hand' now operates globally and with fewer countervailing pressures from governments than for decades. Many commentators are optimistic about the prospects for faster growth and for convergence of incomes and living standards which greater global competition should bring.

---

[12] For E. Todd (1998), globalization is the effect not the cause of the vanishing of nations. His controversial but thought provoking book is a fervent plea for a return to Nation-States and to intelligent protectionism. Todd calls for the denunciation of the Maastricht treaty and is hostile to the independence of central banks. While taking a more balanced view of the globalization processes, I have also argued for the strengthening of Nation-States as a buffer against the negative impacts of globalization (Sachs, 1996 and 1997a).

[13] This is certainly the case of several post-socialist countries which started their transition to market economy under the spell of doctrinaire neoliberalism and minimum State theories, only to learn in a hard way the importance of assigning the right role to the State in the process of transformation, see Chavance, B. (1998).

However, there is also another big story. Since the early 1980s the world economy has been characterized by rising inequality and slow growth. Income gaps between North and South have continued to widen. In 1965, the average per capita income of the G7 countries was 20 times that of the world's poorest seven countries. By 1995 it was 39 times as much'. (UNCTAD, 1997, p. IV).

UNCTAD's Secretary-General, Rubens Ricupero, rightly points out that the present modest rates of growth of about 3 per cent per year—some 2 percentage points lower than that achieved during the 'Golden Age' of 1950–73—can solve neither the North's employment problem nor the South's poverty problem. The more so since the liberalization of the world economy has proceeded in a lopsided way, discriminating against areas in which the South can achieve a comparative advantage.

As for the third crisis mentioned by T. Banuri, it stems from inefficient social control over the development of science and technology, resulting in frequent mismatches between technical progress and genuine people's needs, excessive rates of 'creative destruction' (which becomes wasteful destruction *tout court*) and unnecessarily high social and environmental costs of economic growth. All the attention goes to the Smithian allocative efficiency, to the detriment of Keynesian efficiency (taking full advantage of the growth potential of the economy) and of the Schumpeterian efficiency (the ability to harness technical progress for social advancement).[14]

Institutional and policy innovations that will come of age in the next decades will vary from country to country, given the wide spectrum of actual social, economic, political and environmental configurations. Yet, some common features are likely to prevail. Some among them are discussed below.

A Bright Future for Middle-way Democratic Regimes

A comeback of the extreme models of dogmatic socialism and free-market 'madness' in G. Harcourt's terms (see Chang, H. J., 1997b)

---

[14] For the distinction between the three efficiencies, see Kuttner, R. (op. cit). Ruffolo, G. (1988) provides an interesting analysis of the gap between the technical progress of our civilization and the primitive planning and policy tools. See also Salomon, J. J., F. Sagasti, C. Sachs-Jeantet (eds) (1994).

is highly improbable. That leaves us with the broad family of middle-way democratic regimes, blending 'neo-socialism' and 'neo-capitalism' and transcending the somewhat scholastic opposition between 'social democracy' and 'social liberalism'. In J. Wilheim's words, they should be

capable of reflecting new values, the new social contract and the resulting new governance, the need to reassess the redistribution and the use of time, the needs and quality of life of the urbanized humankind, the new connection between rural and urban systems, the new concepts of education and of democracy.... The perspective of a fascinating new world, the *Renaissance* of the 21st century! If we can make it true.... (Wilheim, J., 1998, p. 103).

The search for third ways has been often derided and dismissed as an impossible utopia. It is submitted, however, that it constitutes a path to explore on the condition of thoroughly analysing the lessons of recent history.

This explains the importance of proceeding towards an exhaustive appraisal of independent India's attempt at charting a 'middle path' under the leadership of J. L. Nehru and P. C. Mahalanobis, by far the most comprehensive experiment of its kind, whatever the judgement on its successes and failures.[15] Rather than mimetically reproducing ready-made blueprints brought from abroad, the challenge is to put to work social imagination to evolve indigenous solutions. These should respond to the singularities of each country, be rooted in its intellectual and political history and, at the same time, take advantage of other countries' experiences, positive and negative. The development potential of a country rests on its cultural ability to formulate a *national project*, then to mobilize the political and administrative capacity to carry it out, much more than on its endowment in natural resources and the degree of advancement of the productive forces, important as they may be. This cannot happen in the absence of *self-confidence* which should not be confused with chauvinistic arrogance and self-congratulation.[16]

---

[15] S. Chakravarty's synthetic book on the Indian experience in development planning (1987) provides a starting point. See also Sachs (1994).

[16] Self-reliance (not to be mixed up with autarky) and self-confidence are to a great extent overlapping concepts insofar as they insist on the autonomous decision-making.

All the middle way regimes operate 'mixed economies' combining in different proportions and configurations the public, the private and the social sectors.

The latter term encompasses all non-profit seeking organized activities together with the cooperative and mutual aid institutions. In Brazil, two partly overlapping concepts are in vogue. The current reform of the State aims at transferring to 'social organizations' belonging to the 'non-State public sector' the management of non-exclusive social services such as hospitals, universities and technical schools, research centres, libraries and museums. The underlying assumption is that the public sphere is broader than the State. When the market is clearly incapable of delivering certain services in a way which guarantees an equitable access to them and the State is over-burdened and/or inefficient, it makes sense to transcend the State market dichotomy and hand over these functions to social organizations (Bresser Pereira, L. C., 1997, pp. 22–31).

On the other hand, the voluntary non-profit organizations are known as the *third sector*, 'private, nevertheless public' (Rubem Cesar Fernandes).[17]

Private sector is a highly heterogenous category encompassing modern enterprises, a broad variety of unregistered small enterprises, family farms and an army of independent producers of goods and providers of services. 'Informal' activities permeate it, but do not constitute a separate sector. As the informal economic agents are, by definition, excluded from the operation of social welfare systems, reverting the present trend towards informality, observed in many developing and developed countries alike, constitutes a *coditio sine qua non* to move towards more equitable socio-economic regimes. The inability to deal with the unemployment problem may be an explanation, but by no means a justification for the complacency towards the swelling of the informal labour markets. The social sector could play a pivotal role in overcoming the informality.[18]

---

[17] 'Third sector stands for all that is neither State nor market and which pursues public interest, non-profit, philanthropic and voluntary endeavours' (Cardoso, Ruth, 1997, p. 7).

[18] For more details, see chapter 5.

Civil Society and Governance: Development Compacts?

The emergence of the self-instituted civil society as an independent social partner will thoroughly modify governance systems. It is too early to say whether the civil society has the potential to become a third system of power, side by side with the political power and the economic power, as suggested in the Third Systems Project of the International Foundation for Development Alternatives and captured in the emblematic title of the celebrated essay by IFDA's president, Marc Nerfin: 'Neither Prince, nor Merchant: the Citizen' (M. Nerfin, 1986). There are, however, good reasons to believe that citizens movements and organizations, distinct from political parties and trade unions, made an irreversible entry on the political scene.

Till date, their presence there has not been sufficiently acknowledged and certainly not adequately institutionalized. Several ambiguities subsist, some cultivated by citizen movements themselves, other by governments.

– Who empowers them? Is it a self-instituted process, or a partial devolution of power on the part of the central authorities, interested in divesting themselves from certain responsibilities? Empowerment, as seen by John Friedmann (1992 and 1996), differs sharply from the views of the communitarians of A. Etzioni's persuasion[19] and has strictly nothing to do with President Reagan's utterances on the subject.

– In which spaces of development will the citizen movements and organizations have their niche? Should they confine themselves to the local space or rather have the ambition (fully justified in my opinion) of acting in all spaces—local, regional, national, international? The unfinished European discussion on

---

[19] As a reaction to excessive individualism and to the preponderance of economic interests, in competition with conservative social movements of a religious nature, communitarians seek the regeneration of the social order based on moral values shared by the community. They advocate work sharing and promotion of community jobs, a multi-partisan agreement to keep the social safety net and voluntary limitation of conspicuous consumption combined with the pursuit of other less material sources of satisfaction (Etzioni, E., 1996, p. 84).

subsidiarity[20] and the worldwide trend towards decentralization are closely related to the above question.

Decentralization is often presented as synonymous with democratization although these two processes are not necessarily germane. Nor is it reasonable to divest the Nation-State of responsibilities that cannot be properly handled at the regional or local level. Therefore, the much needed institutional reforms ought to tackle simultaneously two problems: the proper articulation of all spaces of development[21] and the democratization of *all* levels of governance.

Citizens movements and associations should be, accordingly, given a permanent opportunity to participate in the governance at local, regional and national levels, along side political parties, trade unions and organized business.

In my opinion, such participation could take the form of a permanent quadripartite dialogue and negotiation around development strategies and concerted ways of implementing them, translated into bundles of contracts setting the responsibilities of the stakeholders and adding up into a development compact.

The arguments in support of the above proposal are summarized below:

1. The usefulness of tripartite negotiations is widely acknowledged. There is no reason why *quadripartite* negotiations would not succeed, provided appropriate forums are created to this effect.

At the local (municipal) level they could take the form of development councils, started as a consultative body, with the possibility of later transformation into deliberative organs. Proposals of this kind were formulated after the 1992 UN Conference on Environment and Development in connection with the elaboration of Agendas 21. Very little progress has been achieved since, but the need to move in this direction has been reaffirmed at the June 1997 special session of the UN General Assembly on

---

[20] Who decides on what should be left to the lower echelon and what should move to the upper one?

[21] In Brazil, it implies i.a. a recomposition of the 'federative pact' to ensure a more harmonious relationship between the different regions of the country and, certainly, to curb the disastrous malpractices of 'fiscal wars' between states and municipalities engaged in wooing of foreign and national investors.

Rio+5. Room should be left for experimenting with different kinds of development forums and/or councils, based on a variable territorial geometry (single municipalities or consortia, special administrative units such as extractivist reserves, biosphere reserves, micro-regions, river catchments, etc.).

At regional and national levels, the first step might consist in conferences attended by a large spectrum of stakeholders (what in France is called *Etats généraux*), an occasion not merely to learn about people's demands (*cahiers de doléances*) but also to identify opportunities for action.

2. My expectation is that the third sector will bring into debate and negotiation a greater awareness of the people's problems and aspirations, a more detailed knowledge of diverse local settings and of latent, underutilized or misused resources and manpower,[22] as well as imagination in proposing and designing innovative partnerships with other stakeholders,[23] a subject which figured prominently at the 1996 UN Habitat Conference held in Istanbul. Citizens movements, especially those committed to environmental causes and to the protection of women's and children's rights, are better fit to represent the interests of the future generations than any other stakeholder (see Kothari, R., 1998, pp. 281–2).

The difficult condition to fulfill, however, will be to ensure the appropriate third sector's representation for each discussed subject, both in terms of competence and genuine public support and legitimacy. This will call for considerable institutional flexibility and open-minded experimentation. As already mentioned, the development forums and councils should work with a variable geometry.

I have argued elsewhere (Sachs, 1998b) for the reconceptualization of development in terms of an effective appropriation of human rights, individual and collective, negative (freedom from) and

[22] Insofar as cities are ecosystems and, therefore, resource potentials, eco-development strategies in the urban setting must rely on the identification and harnessing of these resources. See the proceedings of the Seminar on Latin-American Metropolitan Cities Facing the Crisis organized in São Paulo by Jorge Wilheim in 1984 (PMSP/CEPAL/UNU, 1985) and Sachs, I. (1993).

[23] One of the slogans of the 1968 movement in Paris was 'imagination to power'. The first volume of Celso Furtado's memoirs captures the essence of development planning in its suggestive title: *A Fantasia Organisada*.

positive (freedom for): the first-generation political, civil and civic rights, the second-generation economic, social and cultural rights, the third-generation collective rights (city, environment, development). L. C. Bresser Pereira (1998) proposes to add to this list a fourth generation of republican rights, guaranteeing access to and wise use of public patrimonies. Human rights could serve as entry points into the discussion of development strategies, facilitating the organization of quadripartite dialogues and negotiations.

3. The smooth working of democratic middle way regimes requires identifying areas of consensus between stakeholders and, even more importantly, reaching compromises between their often conflicting interests. Continuous negotiation between stakeholders is thus central to the very existence of these regimes. Following the lead of Scandinavian scholars, we may speak of a *negotiated economy* or perhaps of a *negotiated and contractual economy*, as contracts ought to follow successful negotiations.

The theoretical underpinnings of this conceptualization may be found in the writings of neo-institutionalists, regulationists and proponents of the theory of conventions.

More importantly, one may refer to the fairly successful practices of French planning at the time when it still had a meaningful function in the French system of governance. An abundant literature misinterprets it as 'indicative' planning. But the indicative figures contained in successive French plans did not matter much. Plans were unimportant. What really mattered was the *planning process*, carried through working groups composed by experts and by representatives of all social partners. The documents thus produced—white books and reports—reflected a concerted opinion thus offering guidelines for public policies, indications to private actors (enterprises) and substance for the so-called *contrats de plan*, implemented through partnerships between central and local authorities, public and private enterprises and occasionally the third sector.

Wither the State?

We may now map out the main functions assigned to the State in the middle way democratic regimes operating a negotiated and contractual economy. Hopefully, it should be capable of resisting the onslaught of neoliberal doctrines aimed at destroying collective structures staying in the way of unhampered pursuit of egoistic interest and individual passion for profit. Neoliberals propose a minimalist, weak State. The challenge then is to reconstruct a *leaner* but *stronger* State, guardian and promoter of public interest, playing a key role in the emerging new social order based on the rational pursuit by collective bodies (citizens associations, political parties, trade unions) of collectively elaborated and approved objectives (Bourdieu, P., 1998).

A broad agreement exists about the priority to be assigned to *regulatory functions* of the State. Even unconditional supporters of the market economy agree, that too much market kills the market. To function properly, markets need clearly established rules of the game. But it is at best a shallow, if not totally deceptive consensus, insofar as opinions diverge sharply on some fundamental issues, some of which are enumerated below:

- Do we need at present new and better regulation—nationally and internationally—or, on the contrary, accelerated deregulation as suggested by some international bodies?

- What weight should be given to economic and non-economic (legal, administrative) instruments in governing markets?

- More important is how to harmonize the social, environmental and economic concerns? To this effect should we, pretexting efficiency, extend economic rationality to all spheres of public and even private life or, on the contrary, refuse to consider markets as *pars pro toto*, roll back economics to its instrumental (albeit crucially important) place, recognize that 'everything is not for sale' (Robert Kuttner) and reaffirm the primacy of the democratic political process?

One can safely assume that the answers to these questions will vary considerably from country to country, accounting for the different shapes of the various emerging middle way regimes.

An implicit condition for the working of a negotiated economy is the existence of a framework provided by a *national project* evolved through an intense societal (citizen) debate comparing alternative development options[24] seeking a balance between the

---

[24] Planning is 'variant thinking', M. Kalecki used to say. This is by far the most lapidary definition of planning.

ideal and the possible, a 'viable utopia' (Cardoso, F. H., 1998, p. 32) and setting in this way the limits of *responsible voluntarism*. The national project must then be unfolded into a development strategy free from the distortions of 'short termism'—the negative impact on long-term development objectives of short-term trade and financial liberalization policies proposed by the Washington consensus (Nayyar, D., 1998).

Planning plays a pivotal role in the eco-development approach aimed at harmonizing the social, environmental and economic objectives. Yet, it has a bad reputation, nowadays, as the result of the collapse of centrally planned command economies in the Soviet bloc. We certainly need a *very* different type of planning, strategic, flexible,[25] dialogical, oecumenic with respect to the participation of social actors, involving the citizens at large by taking the discussion of options to the public place, contractual.

In the absence of such a planning effort, organized by the State, the stakeholders engaged in the negotiating procedures will act without a clear vision of national priorities in the long term. They will be, furthermore, deprived from a framework allowing for the compatibility of the diverse projects, so as to promote synergies between them instead of costly duplications and negative-sum competitive games.

The regulatory and the planning functions mutually reinforce each other. Institutional design must be attuned to the goals set in the national project. On the other hand, the development options of a country depend to some extent on the adopted regulatory regime.

Should the State also act as a *direct producer* of goods and provider of services?

The current mood favours less State and more market, with a strong bias towards outright privatization of public enterprises. This is a complete reversal of the attitude prevailing in the post-War period marked by a wave of nationalizations, first in Europe, then in the periphery of the capitalist world. The emphasis on

[25] In the Soviet type planning, future uncertainties were so to say exorcised by proceeding to the allocation of the totality of resources for the whole duration of the plan. There was practically no room for adaptation to face contingencies of all sorts. Flexible (and rolling) planning on the contrary, tries, as much as possible, to maintain open options at each point of time, by taking only those decisions needed to keep the economy on the desired path.

privatization of public enterprises should not detract us, however, from the paramount task of *deprivatization of the State* already referred to, which involves getting rid of all the pathologies of statism, patrimonialism, clientelism and crony capitalism.

The main argument advanced in favour of privatization insists on the poor managerial record of public enterprises, as compared with the efficiency and the dynamism of private entrepreneurs. This assertion is often, but by no means always true and calls for empirical verification, case by case.

At any rate, historically the Schumpeterian entrepreneurial function in peripheral countries has been to a great extent performed by the State, not by private entrepreneurs. The private sector does not object to the socialization of initial investment and risk in the infant stage of industrialization, provided it may expect to take over at a later stage, on favourable financial conditions, those enterprises started in the public sector, whose viability has been tested or, else, which operate a natural monopoly.

Streamlining of the public sector is certainly called for, first getting rid of strategically unimportant, money loosing, junk enterprises purchased at some point by the State to rescue their former private owners from bankruptcy (a typical gesture of privatized State). But in countries with a sizeable public sector, where *programmatic nationalizations* were carried out in the past, total withdrawal of the State from productive functions raises several controversial questions.

– Should the State maintain its position in the sectors of the economy considered as 'strategic'? Should it aim at a public monopoly there, or allow for a competition between public and private enterprises?

– Should foreign and national investors be given equal treatment?

– How to proceed with respect to natural monopolies? Which public services, if any, should be directly performed by the State? What should be the regime of concessions for the services framed out to private companies and/or to social organizations? How to involve the users' associations in the management of public services?

Another set of questions refers to State participation in the financial sector.

- What should be the role of public development banks? How should they differ from private investment banks? What kind of concessional (subsidized) financing should they provide to targeted social groups (such as family farmers or small entrepreneurs) as well as to less developed territorial units?

Should the State carry out within the public sector, or through mixed enterprises, projects deemed as priority for which private investment is not forthcoming?[26]

- What should the degree of autonomy of the central bank be in the conduct of monetary policy?

Historically, *research* in developing countries has been a quasi-monopoly of the public sector.

- What is the realistic prospect for greater involvement of the private sector in research? Is it desirable beyond a certain point, given that private research is likely to concentrate on technologies concerning only the enterprises, to the detriment of socially established priorities of research?

- Science and technology ought to be treated as a public good. What does it mean in practical terms in a world in which intellectual property is increasingly privatized and traded as a commodity?[27]

The last set of questions deals with the role of the State as *employer*. The most common form of clientelism consists in creating redundant or even fake employment in public institutions

[26] Of course, private investment can be always persuaded provided the incentives are sufficiently attractive. But beyond a certain point, too generous incentives become self-defeating. The policy question is: where to draw the line?

[27] Ismail Serageldin, vice-president of the World Bank and Chairman of the Consultative Group on International Agricultural Research (CGIAR), rightly attributes the success of the research carried under the auspices of this institution to the implicit contract that the genetic material available in the gene banks was a public resource available for all of humanity. 'All of a sudden we are witnessing a change in the rules of the game, where the best of science is no longer freely available because it is patented, while the genetic collections are still considered public domain'. I fully share his opinion that proprietary science could exacerbate the gap between the haves and the have-nots and that we are running a serious risk of creating a scientific apartheid in the next century (Serageldin, 1998).

at all levels. Overstaffed bureaucracies, exorbitant privileges of the upper strata of public servants, allied to poor performance, generate a very negative image in the eyes of the public who do become receptive to the neoliberal utterances against the State as such. Obviously, these excesses must be curbed.

Yet, somewhat paradoxically, the need is to greatly expand the employment in the public sector, while changing its composition. *Education, health, social services, agriculture extension and environmental protection all require many more personnel.* In Paul Streeten's (1997, p. 68) words:

It is not at all clear that our society cannot use plenty of health-workers, nurses, child rearers, gardeners, plumbers, sweepers, protectors and restorers of the environment, and other service-workers who do not need the high and scarce skills demanded by modern technology and whose services cannot be replaced by either computers or imported low-cost goods from low-income countries (though imported low-cost workers should be welcomed). Many of these jobs are, however, in the currently despised or neglected public sector and may call for even more despised higher taxation. They are also often ill-paid and not recognized as valuable. We need to change our valuation of such work and should guarantee minimum standards of reward for them.

– Should all these jobs be created in the public sector?

– What are the alternative models for the delivery of social services? What kinds of partnerships between the different stakeholders, including the users, are envisageable in these activities?

The questions raised in this paper will receive different answers from one country to another, giving rise to a variety of middle-way regimes and mixed economies. Hopefully, some of them will manage to negotiate innovative development compacts with all the stakeholders.

Reshaping the International Order

The present crisis gives a new urgency to the reshaping of the international order, a subject discussed inconclusively for several decades in many reports,[28] books and conferences. The attempts

---

[28] I have been associated with the preparation of two among these reports: 'What Now?' (1975) and Tinbergen (1976).

by the developing nations in the early seventies to bring about a New International Economic Order was countered by the industrialized countries. Looked at in an historical perspective, the propositions put forward on that occasion lacked the necessary political realism and concreteness. Yet, the agenda identified then is still very much with us. The ongoing globalization processes are likely to sharpen the inequalities within nations and between nations, unless the rules of the game and the interplay of institutions are drastically modified.

The centrality of the UN in the international system should be reaffirmed, reverting the present trend of progressive erosion of its capacity to act due to a lack of sufficient resources among other reasons. This is not likely to happen in the absence of financing of the UN activities through some kind of international taxation, such like the tax on foreign exchange transactions proposed by James Tobin, ocean and air tolls paid by oil tankers and commercial aircraft, a small tax on the 600 million cars circulating at present in the world, etc.

Equally important is a thorough reform of the so-called Bretton Woods institutions, the World Bank and the International Monetary Fund without forgetting the World Trade Organization. The Bank seems aware of the need to reformulate its programmes although it is too early to evaluate the pertinence of the ongoing reform.

The situation is much more serious with respect to the IMF. The mere replenishing of its funds will not in itself solve the problem of redefining the mission of the IMF, in particular its role in the effective regulation of the international financial markets. A complete reversal of policies followed with respect to developing countries, by this institution, is called for.

I also remain quite sceptical about the present role of the WTO. Equity in commercial and economic relations between partners of unequal strength calls for rules of the game biased in favour of the weaker partner. That principle was recognized at the time of creating UNCTAD in the early sixties. Instead, the cornerstone of the WTO is the formal equality among partners. Furthermore, the ongoing privatization of science, technology and culture, actively promoted by the WTO, has far reaching and highly negative consequences on the prospect of development of peripheric countries.

Realistically speaking, the reform of the Bretton Woods institutions will take many years of hard bargaining, the more so that the central economies derive many advantages from the present international (dis)order. The first step in this direction should be putting on the table concrete proposals which, under the circumstances, ought to come primarily from peripheral countries and from scholars identified with their cause. India and Brazil are probably the two countries best suited to make contributions in this respect owing to their political prestige, the competence of their social scientists and the skills of their diplomats.

In parallel, efforts should be renewed to convince the industrialized countries that they ought to seriously consider the economic advantages they might derive from applying 'global Keynesianism'. A larger net transfer of financial resources to the peripheral countries would stimulate their demand for goods and services from central countries (Sunanda Sen, 1998). *Co-development* of North and South could be a mutually advantageous positive-sum game. The case for a 'Marshall plan for the South' can be made not so much by invoking generosity of the rich, but by appealing to their well-understood self-interest. Insofar as the crisis is having a boomerang effect on the economy of the central countries, it may at last paradoxically set the stage for a serious discussion of a *North–South co-development compact*.[29]

References

Albert, M. (1990), *Capitalisme contre capitalisme*, Le Seuil, Paris.

Ayres, R. U. (1998), *Turning Point—An End to the Growth Paradigm*, Earthscan Publications Ltd., London.

Bairoch, P. (1997), *Victoires et déboires—Histoire économique et sociale du monde du XVIe siècle à nos jours*, Gallimard, Paris.

Banque Mondiale, *Rapport sur le Développement dans le Monde 1997, L'Etat dans un monde en mutation*, Washington.

Banuri, Tariq (1998), 'Editorial', *Policy Matters*, nr. 1 (Newsletter of the IUCN Commission on Environmental, Economic and Social Policy).

[29] Parts of this essay were presented as a paper at the Seminar on 'Society and the Reform of the State' organized in São Paulo from 26 to 28 March 1998.

Bhagwati, J. (1998), 'The Capital Myth—The Difference between Trade in Widgets and Dollars', *Foreign Affairs*, vol. 77, no. 3, May–June, New York.

Block, F. (1994), 'The Role of the State in the Economy' in Smelser, N. J. and Swedberg, R. (eds), *The Handbook of Economic Sociology*, Princeton University Press, Princeton.

Bourdieu, P. (1998), 'L'essence du néolibéralisme', *Le Monde Diplomatique*, mars.

Bresser Pereira, L. C. (1997), 'State Reform in the 1990s: Topic and Control Mechanisms', Cadernos Marc, Brasilia.

———— (1998), 'Citizenship and *Res Publica*: the Emergence of Republican Rights', Brasilia (mimeo).

Cardoso, F. H. (1998), 'L'utopie et le politique: du professeur au président', in *Economies et Sociétés—Développement, croissance et progrès*, Série F, n° 36, 1/1998, Presses Universitaires de Grenoble, Grenoble, pp. 29–35.

Cardoso, Ruth (1997), 'Fortalecimento da Sociedade Civil', in Ioschpe, E-B (ed.), *3° Setor Desenvolvimento Social Sustantado*, Paz e Terra, São Paulo, pp. 7–12.

Chakravarty, S. (1987), *Development Planning—The Indian Experience*, Clarendon Press, Oxford.

Chang, H. J. and Rowthorn, R. (eds), (1995), *The Role of the State in Economic Change*, Clarendon Press, Oxford.

Chang, H. J. (1997a), 'The Economics and Politics of Regulation', *Cambridge Journal of Economics*, vol. 21, no. 6, November.

———— (1997b), 'Markets, Madness and Many Middle Ways—Some reflections on the institutional diversity of capitalism' in Arestis, Ph. Palma, G., Sawyer, M. (eds), *Markets, Unemployment and Economic Policy Essays in Honour of Geoff Harcourt*, vol. II, Routledge, Londres and New York, pp. 30–42.

Chavance, B. (1998), 'Grand-route et chemin de traverse de la transformation post-socialiste', *Economies et sociétés—Développement, croissance et progrès*, Série F, n° 36, 1/1998, Presses Universitaires de Grenoble, Grenoble, pp. 141–9.

Crouch, C. and Streeck, W. (sous la direction) (1996), *Les capitalismes en Europe*, La Découverte, Paris.

Deane, P. (1989), *The State and the Economic System*, Oxford University Press, Oxford.

Drucker, P. (1998), 'Beyond Capitalism', *New Perspectives Quarterly*, vol. 15, nr. 2, Spring, pp. 4–12.

Etzioni, A. (1996), *The New Golden Rule. Community and Morality in a Democratic Society*, Basic Books, New York.

Fitoussi, J. P. and Rosanvallon, P. (1996), *Le Nouvel Age des Inégalités*, Le Seuil, Paris.

Friedmann, J. (1992), *Empowerment—The Politics of Alternative Development*, Blackwell, Cambridge, MA & Oxford, UK.

————(1996), 'Rethinking Poverty: Empowerment and Citizen Rights', *International Social Science Journal*, no. 148, UNESCO, June.

Gray, J. (1998), Interview granted to Adriana Chiarini from *Isto É* (São Paulo, Brésil), 7 October.

Group of Lisbon, The (Petrella, R. et al.) (1993), *Limits to Competition*. Gulbenkian Foundation, Lisbon.

Hobsbawm, E. (1994), *The Age of Extremes—A History of the World, 1914–1998*, Pantheon Books, New York.

Kissinger, H. (1998), 'The IMF's Remedies are Doing More Harm than Good', *International Herald Tribune*, London, 5 October.

Kothari, R. (1998), 'Sustainable Development—An Ethical Utopia for the 21st Century', *Economies et Sociétés—Développement, croissance et progrès*. Série F, n° 36, 1/1998, Presss Universitaires de Grenoble, Grenoble, pp. 279–86.

Kozul-Wright, R. (1995), 'The Myth of Anglo-Saxon Capitalism: Reconstructing the History of the American State', in Chang, H. J. and Rowthorn, R. (eds), pp. 81–113.

Krugman, P. (1998), 'E hora de ser radical com a crise da Ásia, *O Estado de São Paulo*, 30 de Agosto.

Kumarappa, J. C. (1950), *The Gandhian Economy and Other Essays*, Magarwadi, Wardha.

Kurien, C.T. (1997), 'Development with Equity', *Economic and Political Weekly*, 10 May.

Kuttner, R. (1997), *Everything for Sale, the Virtues and Limits of Markets*, Alfred A. Knopf, New York.

Nerfin, M. (1986) 'Neither Prince nor Merchant: Citizen—An Introduction to the Third System', *IFDA Dosier*, n° 56, novembre–décembre, pp. 3–29. Reprinted in *Development Dialogue*, 1987, nr. 1, pp. 170–95.

Nayyar, D. (1998), 'Short-termism, Public Policies and Economic Development', *Economies et Sociétés—Développement, croissance et progrès*. Série F, n° 36, 1/1998, Presses Universitaires de Grenoble, Grenoble, pp. 107–18.

Prefeitura de São Paulo/CEPAL/UNU (1985), *América Latina: Crise nas Metropoles*, São Paulo.

Presidency of the Republic, State Reform Committee (1995), *White Paper Reform of the State Apparatus*, Brasilia.

Ruffolo, G. (1988), *Potenza e Potere*, La fluttuazione gigante dell'Occidente, Laterza, Bari.

Sachs, I. (1993), *Transition Strategies towards the 21st Century*, Research and Information System for the Non-Aligned and Other Developing Countries, Interest Publications, New Delhi.

———— (1994), 'L'inde et l'actualité des voies médianes', *Economie Appliquée*, tome XLVII, n° 2, pp. 181–9.

———— (1998b), 'O desenvolvimento enquanto apropriação dos direitos humanos', *Estudos Avançados* 12 (33), São Paulo.

Salomon, J. J., Sagasti, F., Sachs-Jeantet, C. (eds) (1994), *The Uncertain Quest—Science, Technology and Development*, United Nations University Press, Tokyo.

Sen. S. (1998), *Finance and Development* (R. C. Dutt Lectures on Political Economy, 1994), Orient Longman, Calcutta.

Serageldin, I. (1998), Interview granted to *Newsweek*, August 24, p. 52.

Streeten, P. (1997), 'Some Reflections on Social Exclusion' in Gore, C. and Figueiredo, J. B. (eds), *Social Exclusion and Anti-Poverty Policy—A Debate*, IILS–ILO/UNDP, New York, Geneva, pp. 66–73.

Stiglitz, J. E. (1998), *More Instruments and Broader Goals: Moving toward the Post—Washington Consensus* (WIDER Annual Lectures 2), UNU/WIDER, Helsinki.

Tinbergen, J. (under the direction of) (1976), *Reshaping the International Order* (Rio), a Report of the Club of Rome, E. P. Dutton, New York.

Todd, E. (1998), *L'illusion économique*, Gallimard, Paris.

UNCTAD, *Trade and Development Report* (1997), United Nations, New York and Geneva.

'What Now'? (1975), Dag Hammarskjöld Report on Development and International Cooperation, *Development Dialogue*, nr. 1/2, Uppsala.

Wilheim, J. (1998), 'Challenges for Planning in the Present Transitional Period', *Economies et Sociétés—Développement, croissance et progrès*, Série F, n° 38, 1/1998, Presses Universitaires de Grenoble, Grenoble, pp. 99–105.

Ziegler, J., en collaboration avec Mühlhoff, U. (1998), *Les seigneurs du crime—Les nouvelles mafias contre la démocratie*, Le Seuil, Paris.

Negotiated and Contractual Management of Biodiversity

Peoples matter first, as Michael Cernea (1986) would put it, or in John Friedmann's (1996) terms, peoples' rights to livelihood matter first.

My argument is predicated on the centrality of development, understood as the historical process of universal appropriation by people of the totality of human rights, individual and collective, negative (freedom from) and positive (freedom for). By this, I mean the three generations of rights: political, civic and civil; social, economic and cultural, as well as the collective rights to development, to environment and to the city (see Bobbio, M., 1990 and Lafer, C., 1994).

Friedmann's decalogue of rights[1] to livelihood cuts across several individual and collective rights forming the basis of a new social contract that the State should honour before addressing other claims.

In this perspective, then, economic growth is no longer regarded as the blind pursuit of growth for its own sake, but as an expansion of the productive forces of society for the purpose of achieving full citizen rights by the entire population.

[1] Professionally assisted birth, a safe and secure life space, an adequate diet, affordable health care, a good, practical education, political participation, an economically productive life, protection against unemployment, a dignified old age, a decent burial (Friedmann, J., 1996, p. 169).

This refers to people who are our contemporaries, with whom we travel together in the Earthship, but also to all future generations to come (Kothari, Rajni, 1998). The ecologization of thought proposed by Edgar Morin requires expanding the geographic horizon so as to encompass the whole planet, if not the universe, and to contemplate the very long *durée*, in fact, the whole process of co-evolution, of our species with the planet on which it lives. Modern ecology is to a great extent an analysis of the interaction of the natural history with human history, as can be seen from Botkin's *Discordant Harmonies* (1990).

We are, thus, bound by a double ethical imperative: the synchronic solidarity with the present generation and the diachronic solidarity with the future generations. Some, like Kothari, add a third ethical concern, the respect for the sanctity of nature:

Respect of nature's diversity, and the responsibility to conserve that diversity, define sustainable development as an ethical ideal. Out of an ethics of respect for nature's diversity flows a respect for the diversity of cultures and livelihoods, the basis not only of sustainability, but also of justice and equity (p. 285).

Biodiversity conservation enters the scene, once we take this very long and broad look at the future of the humankind. To ensure the rights of future generations, biodiversity must be protected.

This is not to say, however, that protection should take exclusively the form of inviolable sanctuaries, even though the need for a network of protected areas may be necessary as part of *aménagement du territoire*. Two caveats are in order here.

– *Wilderness*, nature without people, is a concept present in American conservationist thought. In most parts of the world, however, it is myth (Diegues, A. C., 1996), as it abstracts from the forest people. What we believe to be a primeval forest, has been in reality profoundly altered by human presence and, sometimes, enriched, as documented by archeological research in the Amazon region. Even more importantly, we ought to remember that more than 60 million tribal people live in the forests of India.

– Multiplying reserves without having the necessary means to protect them effectively is a self-defeating policy. People removed from the reserves, or prevented from entering there to collect forest products on which they have always depended, consider this to be a violation of their right to livelihood. They react by encroaching the reserves which, in this way, become for all practical purposes open access areas, *res nullius*, an easy prey for looting.

Without falling into the kind of epistemological optimism and unlimited faith in the technological fix, epitomized in the writings of Julian Simon, I stay with Hubert Reeves when he says that human beings are 'the most complex and the most performing product of the nature' (p. 147). The word 'performing' denotes here the capability of affecting in a significant way the environment, for the best or for the worst. As an intelligent species with a remarkable adaptive capacity, we ought to be able to invent an *economy of permanence*, as proposed by J. C. Kumarappa, a disciple of Gandhi. In the economy of permanence, satisfaction of genuine human needs, self-limited to avoid greed, goes hand in hand with conservation of biodiversity. A symbiosis between humans and nature (Serres, Michel, 1990) is thus achieved. Over millennia we have learned how to transform natural ecosystems into fields and gardens, which are sustainable when conveniently managed. By putting to contribution contemporary science we can envisage a new form of civilization, based on a sustainable use of renewable resources. The well-known Indian scientist M. S. Swaminathan considers it not only possible but essential.

The economy of permanence should be predicated on *resource-fulness*, the ability to transform into resources elements of the environment, without destroying the capital of nature. Resource is a cultural and historical concept, the knowledge of a society on the potentialities of its environment. Is resource today what was not resource yesterday; some of the resources on which we rely today will be discarded tomorrow; so goes the technical progress.

We should rely, as much as possible, on the flow of renewable resources. However, renewability of resources, meaning by this term the basic life supports—water, soils, climates—require an ecologically prudent management, it is not an attribute given to them once forever.

In other words, we must learn how to make a *wise use of nature* to build a *good society* (Larrède, Catherine et Raphael, 1997). Conservation of biodiversity is a necessary condition of sustainable development, as recognized by the Earth Summit and enshrined in the biodiversity convention. And, reciprocally, as we shall see later on, eco-development constitutes an appropriate way of conserving biodiversity, probably the most appropriate one as it allows for harmonizing social and ecological objectives.

A few words on sustainability are in order here.[2] Often, the term is used to denote environmental sustainability. I believe, however, that this concept has several other dimensions. Let me briefly enumerate them:

– social sustainability comes first, as it overlaps with the very finality of development, not speaking of the probability that social collapse may happen before environmental catastrophe,

– a corollary: cultural sustainability;

– environmental sustainability comes next;

– it also has a corollary: a balanced territorial distribution of human settlements and activities;

– economic sustainability appears as a necessary but, by no means a sufficient condition of the previous ones, as economic disruption brings about social disruption, which in turn hampers environmental sustainability;

– the same can be said of lack of political governance; hence the paramount importance of political sustainability to steer the harmonization process reconciling development with biodiversity conservation;

– again, a corollary comes here: the sustainability of the international system to maintain peace—modern wars are not only genocides but also ecocides—and to evolve a governance system for the common heritage of humankind.

I shall now discuss the conservation of biodiversity through eco-development. Under this name, India is carrying out several projects around tiger reserves and in national parks with active support of Global Environment Fund. Eco-development is defined in these projects as 'a strategy for protecting ecologically valuable areas (protected areas) from unsustainable or otherwise unacceptable pressures resulting from the needs and activities of people living in and around such areas' (Singh, S., 1997, p. 48). It attempts to this by three means:

[2] For more details see chapter 2.

– identifying, establishing and developing sustainable alternatives for biomass resources and incomes;

– involving the people living in and around protected areas into the conservation planning and management of the area;

– raising the levels of awareness, among the local community of the value and conservation needs of the protected area and of patterns of sustainable growth locally appropriate.

Eco-development thus requires site-specific, micro-level, participatory planning involving the protected area authority, the village communities and the citizens associations. For more radical writers, it also calls for the recognition of the legitimate resource rights and needs of local communities, giving them a central role in planning, protection and monitoring of protected areas and allowing for a healthy interaction between folk knowledge and modern science (see Kothari et al., 1995).

I could also quote the pioneering experiences in Madagascar and the research conducted there by Jacques Weber and the research group GREEEN/CIRAD (Weber, J., 1994 and Sachs, I. and Weber, J., 1997), as well as the South–South Co-operation Programme on Environmentally Sound Socio-Economic Development in the Humid Tropics (UNESCO/MAB–UNU–TWAS–UNAMAZ).

The latter works on eco-development of the buffer and transition zones in the so-called biosphere reserves, where controlled human activities are admitted. What is valid there applies *a fortiori* in situations where environmental restrictions are less strict.

Moreover, by putting together people working in different countries where similar ecosystemic conditions prevail, the environmental variable is so to say put outside the bracket. What remains inside the bracket is their cultural diversity. In this way, research on biodiversity and research on cultural diversity become closely related. It is to be hoped that this programme will be replicated one day for other ecosystems, so as to explore the ecosystems/cultures matrix more systematically. Read horizontally, this matrix shows the cultural diversity of responses to similar environmental challenges. Read vertically, it gives us an insight into the adaptability of one culture to different natural conditions.

Many more examples could be cited, particularly in India. Participatory planning on an unprecedented scale has been attempted in the state of Kerala, and pioneering experiences of setting up panchayat biodiversity registers, started in Karnataka, are spreading to other states.

A common experience is that eco-development can be best achieved by resorting to customary resource management systems and by organizing a participatory process of identification of needs, resource potentials and ways of using the biodiversity in a way which improves the peoples' livelihoods. This process calls for the presence of *advocacy planners* of one kind or another, who act as facilitators of the negotiation process between the stakeholders— local populations and authorities, assisted by scientists, extentionists and civic associations, economic agents, both private and public. These negotiations are often painful because of antagonistic interests, as shown in a recent study of challenges to community-based sustainable development. Nevertheless, they represent a welcome departure from earlier approaches to environmental management (Leach, M. et alii, 1997).

To succeed, it is, however, necessary to transform the results of the negotiation into a *contract* between the stakeholders. We may thus speak of a *negotiated and contractual management of resources*, as the cornerstone of any sustainable development.[3]

An important condition is to ensure that local people will effectively have their share of the benefits resulting from the uses of their knowledge and of the genetic resources collected by them. They must be protected from biopiracy. This is a very tall order indeed. The evolution of the whole debate on the intellectual property has gone, as we know, the wrong way. This question will loom very large in the implementation of the biodiversity convention.

The negotiated and participatory approach is crucially important in sensitive areas such as tropical forests. But it can also be fruitfully applied in the context of developed economies.

An interesting example is provided by the 33 French Natural Regional Parks which cover approximately 10 per cent of the national territory with a population of over two and half million people involving over 2700 communes. Their name is to some extent misleading, insofar as these are micro-regions with fragile ecosystems or else important natural or historical heritage, whose

---

[3] See on this point M. Jollivet et al. (1997).

inhabitants have negotiated among them a charter defining the development objectives and the modalities of their implementation. The charters are negotiated for a period of 10 years among representatives of communes, departments and regions with the participation of citizens organizations. A mixed syndicate of the communes participating in the Park is entrusted with its management. The Parks celebrated 30 years of their existence last year. They can be seen as forerunners of eco-development,[4] even though the citizens organizations ought to have a larger role. The question now is how to profit from the accumulated experience of contractual participative management in areas that have not been singled out as national parks. A step in this direction may take the form of territorial charters co-signed by several communes.

To conclude, the negotiated and contractual approach goes far beyond the management of biodiversity. I have argued in chapter six that it could become the cornerstone of democratic middle-way regimes, as a creative response to the present crisis of paradigms—the collapse of real socialism, the running out of steam of welfare states, the unfulfilled promises of the neoliberal counter-revolution (Sachs, 1998). But that is another story.

References

Bobbio, N. (1990), *L'eta dei Diritti*, Giulio Einaudi Editore, Torino.

Botkin, D. B. (1990), *Discordant Harmonies: A New Ecology for the 21st Century*, Oxford University Press, Oxford.

Cernea, M. M. (ed.) (1986), 'Putting People First: Sociological Variables in Rural Development', World Bank, Technical Paper 80, Washington, D. C.

Diegues, A. C., Sant'Ana (1996), *O Mito Moderno da Natueza intocada*, Hucitec, São Paulo.

Friedmann, J. (1996), 'Rethinking Poverty: Empowerment and Citizen Rights', *International Social Science Journal*, nr. 148, pp. 161–72.

Jollivet, M., Legay, J. M. and Mégie, G. (1997), 'Vers un développement négocié?', *Natures, Sciences et Sociétés*, vol. 5, n°3.

Kothari, A., Suri, S. and Singh, N. (1995), 'People and Protected Areas. Rethinking Conservation of India', *The Ecologist*, vol. 25, no. 5.

---

[4] See, in particular, their Manifesto (Parcs Naturels Régionaux, 1997) presented in June 1997 during the festivities of the thirtieth anniversary.

Kothari R. (1998), 'Sustainable Development—An Ethical Utopia for the 21st Century', *Economies et Sociétés—Développement, croissance et progrès.* Série F nr. 36, 1/1998, pp. 279–86.

Lafer, C. (1992), 'A reconstrução dos direitos humanos'. Um dialogo com o pensamento de Hannah Arendt, Companhia das Lettras, São Paulo.

Larrède, C. et R. (1997), *Du bon usage de la nature*, Aubier, Paris.

Leach, M., Mearns, R. and Scoones, I. (1997), 'Community-Based Sustainable Development—Consensus or Conflict?', *IDS Bulletin*, vol. 28, no. 4.

Parcs Naturels Régionaux de France (1997), *Manifeste pour un futur durable.*

Reeves, H. (1990), *Malicorne—Réflexions d'un observateur de la nature*, Editions du Seuil, Paris.

Sachs, I. and Weber, J. (1997), 'Developing in Harmony with Nature: Guidelines for Resource Management by People in the Biosphere Reserves', in Aragon, L. E. and Clüsener-Godt, M. (eds), *Reservas da Biosfera e Reservas Extrativistas: Conservação da Biodiversidade e Ecodesenvolvimento*, UNAMAZ–UNESCO, Belem, pp. 9–20.

Sachs, I. (1998), 'The State and the Social Partners: Towards a Development Compact', Paper Prepared for the Seminar on Society and the Reform of the State, São Paulo, 26–8 March.

Serres, M. (1990), *Le contrat naturel*, François Bourin, Paris.

Singh, S., (1997), 'Biodiversity Conservation Through Eco-development. Planning and Implementation: Lessons from India' in Aragon, L. E. and Clüsener-Godt, M. (eds), *Reservas da Biosfera e Reservas Extrativistas: Conservação da Biodiversidade e Ecodesenvolvimento*, UNAMAZ-UNESCO, Belem, pp. 21–90.

Weber, J. (1994), 'Les relations entre populations et aires protégées à Madagascar', *Nature, Sciences et Sociétés*, n° 2.

Citizenhood: Local, National, Regional and Planetary

A hundred and fifty years ago, the *Communist Manifesto* rightly diagnosed capitalism's compulsion to create, dominate and exploit world markets. Globalization has been advancing since then by ups and downs. Its scope and depth are maximum in the financial realm and in communication. Its grip is much weaker on production, employment and even trade. According to Gauron (1998, p. 75–6), the 40,000 transnational corporations (TNCs) identified by the United Nations account for only 8 per cent of world GNP. European exports to the rest of the world are stagnating at 8.6 per cent of the European GNP, while European imports to the rest of the world's decreased from 9.8 to 8.7 per cent between 1960 and 1996. It is safe to assume that over 90 per cent of the world's global workforce is employed in activities oriented towards the internal markets.

This is not to minimize the impact of the financial globalization nor the growing relative share of TNCs intra trade in world commerce. Lack of adequate international and national controls on huge instant flows of capital around the globe round the clock introduces a structural instability in the world economy, manifesting itself through recurrent financial crises. The Asian crisis is the most recent, but most probably not the last one. Far from homogenizing the world economy, financial globalization reinforces the domination of a handful of countries and expands the disparities between rich and poor, within and between nations. At the same time, TNCs are the main winners in international trade.

Globalization is, thus, a complex historical process which, in its present form, produces few winners and many losers. The situation is worsened by the fact that this particular form of globalization is presented as the only possible and unavoidable one. Communication comes in here. We are all exposed to a powerful propaganda of sorts, carried out through the world's media, distorting the real picture of the world economy, occulting its slowdown since the advent of the neoliberal conservative revolution, insisting on the present form of globalization as the best one, undermining by all possible means the State as an obstacle in its way, preaching a new social order based on the tyranny of the market and the pre-eminence of the global economic forces, side by side with the exaltation of local democracy. The neoliberal gospel is based on a kind of economistic fatalism which Bourdieu (1998) compares to the Marxist economistic fatalism. Both demobilize and annihilate the realm of politics and introduce an unacceptable separation between the economic and the social realms.[1]

We are clearly in the presence of a new ideology, which might be called *globalism* as opposed to genuine *internationalism* and *universalism*. Globalism must, of course, be resisted, insofar as it purports to destroy the Welfare States painfully built after the Second World War in the industrialized countries and undermines the international order in which the relations between North and South were supposed to reflect equity and not formal reciprocity. UNCTAD was built on the principle that to be equitable the rules of the game must be biased in favour of weak partners; this is no longer the case with the WTO. Instead we need *globalization with a human face*—a goal put forward by the parties of the Socialist International, which intend to launch a political initiative to this effect. The two pillars of such a globalization ought to be the values of universalism and internationalism.

By universalism I understand the values enshrined in the Universal Declaration of Rights. In general, I believe that development can be reconceptualized in terms of effective appropriation of the totality of human rights regrouped in three 'generations':

- the political, civil and civic rights;

[1] Economistic fatalism characterized the vulgar Marxists which must be contrasted with the views of Marx himself, who always recognized the importance of politics.

– the social, economic and cultural rights;
– the collective rights to development, to environment, to the city.[2]

It is understood that the beneficiaries of these rights ought to assume the responsibilities attached to them fully participating in the conduct of public affairs. In other words, development can be seen as the process of universalizing and expanding the *citizenhood*,[3] the positive contents of democracy.

Internationalism stands here for commitment to equity between nations and is closely linked to the principles of solidarity and responsibility for the well-being of present and future generations. While this term has been monopolized by the communist movement for many years, there is no reason to abandon it. On the contrary, it must be given new content and strength.

Historically, citizenhood was born in ancient Greek cities, as can be seen from the etymology of this word. It certainly has a local dimension which must be upheld by all means. There is room for expanding direct democracy and participatory management based on negotiation among all *stakeholders* leading to contractual arrangements between them.

However, the main space of modern citizenhood is constituted by the Nation-States whose legitimacy and usefulness is being contested by globalism. The very notion of citizenhood, as we understand it today, is inseparable from the working of the State of Right and of the Welfare State. Bourdieu (op. cit.) is right in saying that the main priority for citizens movements today is to oppose the withering of the State although the functions hitherto assumed by the national State may be implemented equally well, or even better, by a supranational State, so long as it remains relatively autonomous with respect to international economic forces, as well as to national political forces and proves capable of developing the social dimension of supranational institutions.

These remarks were made in the context of Europe, but they can be generalized. The same author makes a strong plea for a new internationalism as a counterweight to the nationalist revival

---

[2] For more details, see Sachs (1998b).

[3] As distinct from citizenship which denotes the formal belonging to a nation, but does not say anything about the positive contents of *citoyenneté*.

looming in European politics; trade unions and citizens movements are gathered to unite their forces in the struggle for a social Europe.

Bourdieu's stance is representative of a fairly wide current of opinion in France which challenges the present trend towards the Europe of markets and postulates a different model for the European Union.[4]

This is not the place to discuss the future of Europe, except for asking whether the regional space is a pertinent dimension for the unfolding of citizenhood.

The authors quoted here all seem to consider that, to be effective, European citizenhood ought to give Europeans something more than what they already get through their respective citizenships. Gauron makes a plea in favour of an expanded *European Bill of Rights*, a citizenhood compact. At the same time, he makes it clear that full employment, a major goal, will not be reached in Europe unless it acquires in the European construction the same status as competition and price stability. It is necessary to invert the hierarchy of goals between employment and stability. He also sharply criticizes the European Court for instituting a supranational legal order establishing 'the market totalitarianism' (op. cit. p. 130). Gauron, like Bourdieu, is a partisan of the supranational State, as without the State there is no way to define the general interest; only private interest, regulated by the law of competition subsists.

Even assuming that Europe will be able to generate a meaningful European citizenhood, the danger of *regionalism* will not be dispelled. Looked at from the rest of the world, Europe still is the 'fortress Europe' with its highly protected agriculture and limited exchanges with the outer world. Planetary citizenhood will not be within reach if the world organizes itself in the form of competing regional blocks.

Yet, it is crucially important to move in this direction. To give to citizenhood its full dimension, it is necessary to combine the three spaces: local, national and planetary. The concept of planetary citizenhood may seem farfetched, yet we cannot envisage

[4] See Gauron (op.cit.) and Todd (1998). The latter author considers that globalization, far from dissolving nations, is the product of the self-dissolution of nations. He makes, therefore, a strong plea for the renewed belief in the idea of nation. Is this the nationalist revival feared by Bourdieu?

the future without attempting its construction. In what follows, I briefly discuss four building blocs of planetary citizenhood.

1. Global security comes first, going beyond the mere absence of war. The different dimensions of security (starting with food security) ought to be spelled out and made into the central goal of a reinvigorated UN system. Three aspects of the UN reform seem particularly relevant:

– in its present form, the UN is an intergovernmental agency; other stakeholders in the development process—the organized civil society, but also the economic forces[5]—ought to have a greater say in its decision-making process;

– the political instances of the reinforced UN system should have an effective control not only on all UN agencies but also on the international banks, the IMF and the WTO,[6]

– the independence of the UN system would be greatly enhanced if it could derive its resources from an automatic financing system, be it a kind of world fiscality or putting to economic use the international commons on an ecologically sound basis. These two points are treated below.

2. Bringing under effective regulation the international financial markets is a *conditio sine qua non* for moving towards 'globalization with a human face'. The single most important step in this direction would be the adoption of the Tobin tax on all foreign exchange transactions. Besides reducing the speculative flows of capital, such a tax would yield a very substantial revenue: a tax of 0.1 per cent would bring 166 billion dollars per year! Of course, one can start with a lower rate and even so multiply the resources available at present for international development-oriented action, freeing the UN from painful and paralyzing fund raising. On the initiative of Ignacio Ramonet, an international ONG—ATTAC[7]— has been created recently to foster this idea.

[5] In Marc Nerfin's terms, the citizens and the merchants should join the princes. In Nerfin's analysis, the workers and their trade unions are included in the organized civil society.

[6] A less important question which also calls for streamlining is the present imbalance between the research capability of the UN system, on the one hand, and the World Bank, on the other.

[7] Action pour une Taxe Tobin Au service des Citoyens. ATTAC's Internet site is: http//Attac.org

The Tobin tax should be complemented by internal measures taken at the level of Nation-States, while the functions of the IMF should be redefined in such a way as to give it a more active role in the regulation of international financial markets.

3. Since the Stockholm Conference of Human Environment and Development in 1972, little progress has been accomplished in designing a management system for international commons subordinated to the twin goals of environmental sustainability and wise economic use in the benefit of the good planetary society. The conventions signed at the 1992 Earth Summit in Rio de Janeiro are, at best, a small beginning. But the emphasis on creating markets for trading pollution permits signals a dangerous drift towards future privatization of all world resources, a kind of gigantic planetary enclosure. A bolder vision, rehabilitating the concept of common heritage of the humankind, is required. The matter is relatively urgent. In a recent editorial, the Indian magazine, *Down to Earth* (April 15, 1998) reminded us that the discovery of water on the moon will make it possible to set up a colony there. The absence of a moon pact leaves the way open for the commercial exploitation of lunar mineral wealth. Will it be a repeat of the East India Company? The situation with respect to the sea-bed mineral nodules is not satisfactory either.

Why couldn't all these potential resources be mobilized to fund a concerted international development action? More immediately, instituting ocean and air tolls might provide an easy source of funding for such an action.

4. The concerted international development action could take the form of a North–South codevelopment compact[8] established through a quadripartite negotiation between the representatives of the States, citizens organizations, organized business and trade unions under the auspices of the UN. Considerable ground work, estimating the required flows of resources, has been accomplished during the preparation of the Earth Summit. Of course, updating is required.

The negotiation of a North–South codevelopment compact would be greatly facilitated if the developing countries were to engage in the elaboration of national development compacts based

[8] No resemblance with the 20:20 compact proposed in 1995 by the UNDP.

on the same principle of quadripartite dialogue sponsored by a leaner but stronger State, as a guardian and promoter of public interest, playing a key role in the emerging new social order. (see Sachs, 1998a).

The industrialized countries have a doubly important role to play in this game. They should, of course, cope with the financial burden involved, which they can easily afford.

More significantly, they should take the initiative of questioning and challenging their own development models, unsustainable in the long run and incompatible with an equitable globalization. The developing countries should be dissuaded from trying to follow our patterns of unbridled consumerism, the safest way for them to produce apartheid societies in which only a minority accedes to Western consumption standards. For that, we must give the rest of the world the example of moving away from these wasteful patterns and charting new, socially more equitable and environmentally more prudent, development paths. Before we give our advice to developing countries, we must respond to the Gandhian question: 'how much is enough' for us? This is the only acceptable way of giving lessons to others and a tenet of democratic political culture.

References

Bourdieu, P. (1998), *Contre-feux*, Liber—Raisons d'Agir, Paris.

Gauron, A. (1998), *Le malentendu européen*, Hachette, Paris.

Nerfin, M. (1986), 'Neither Prince Nor Merchant: Citizen', *IFDA Dossier* n° 56, novembre-décembre.

Sachs, I. (1998a), 'The State and the Social Partners: Towards a Development Compact', Paper Prepared for the Seminar 'Society and the Reform of the State', São Paulo, 26–8 March.

——— (1998b), 'O desenvolvimento enquanto apropriação dos direitos humanos', *Estudos Avançados* 12 (33), and 'Lo sviluppo e i diritti dell'uomo', *Relazioni Internazionali* 44, Maggio-Giugno, ISPI.

Todd, E. (1998), *L'illusion économique—essai sur la stagnation des sociétés développées*, Gallimard, Paris.

9

Conclusion: A North–South Dialogue on the Challenges of the 21st Century[1]

On the occasion of the 1992 Indian Science Congress, a group of distinguished scholars set out to explore the interconnectivities and action possibilities related to science, population and development. Their effort culminated in a book (Gowariker, V. (ed.) 1993), now in its third edition, centred around three broad topics:

– the prospect for the demographic transition in India conditioned by a real social and economic transition;

– a sober assessment of the challenge represented by the need to satisfy on a sustainable basis, sometime in the second half of the twenty-first century, the needs of a stationary Indian population of 1.6 to 1.8 billion—*the inevitable billion plus*, even if there are reasons to believe that the rate of fertility will go down sharply in the next decade or two;

– the contribution expected from scientists capable of blending *techne* and *episteme*, the popular know-how and the most advanced science.

The joint effort of the authors unfolds a strategy of sustainable development for India, but why only India? Such a strategy has

[1] This text draws heavily on the article in collaboration with Vasant Gowariker (see Sachs, I., 1994).

many basic ingredients which would be just as applicable elsewhere. In a similar vein, but on a much larger scale, was the stimulus provided by the 1992 Earth Summit, held in Rio de Janeiro, to reflect, on a planetary scale, on ways to promote smooth transitions towards socially equitable, ecologically viable and economically efficient development paths.

For such a transition, it is necessary for the North and the South to recognize their distinct responsibilities and to design, in both groups of countries, different yet synergistic strategies though this is easier said than done.[2]

The whole world must finally grapple with the Gandhian question: 'How much is enough?' The answer to be arrived at would have to be viable in terms of sustainability and eventually applicable universally to be of real practical value. The North just would not be able to continue to be as profligate as it is at present and must begin by making the transition from its present life and consumption styles by shifting to less energy-intensive resource-use patterns. Establishing an equitable trade pattern between the North and the South, transferring of resources from North to South to reverse the present trend of a net outflow of resources from the South to the North, as well as making certain environmentally friendly northern technologies freely available at non-commercial, reasonable prices are three additional important dimensions.

As for the South, it ought to recognize the patently non-viable nature of Northern patterns with at least two criteria of sustainable development mentioned above—social equity and environmental viability—even for the North. Through imitation the South may only expect to recreate enclaves of Northern-style modernity for the benefit of a minority and at the expense of the majority. Hence the need for both the North and the South to steer on newer and original development paths, informed by a more egalitarian vision of the society and a different hierarchy of needs—another Gandhian question. Henceforth, further advances in the North and development in the South should rely, as much as possible, on a resourceful use of renewable resources. A biomass-based modern civilization is not only possible but necessary (M. S. Swaminathan) and in this respect, tropical countries have a comparative advantage.

[2] See Sachs, I. (1993).

India's contributions to the search of a planetary strategy will matter for a variety of reasons:

– almost one in every five citizens of the world will be an Indian;

– the country has a solid ethical and intellectual tradition of looking for an original development path, while maintaining an open dialogue with the rest of the world; at a moment when the South, the North and the East all experience an urgent need to overhaul their failed or exhausted models, India's post-Independence refusal to apply ready-made solutions and her bold attempt at pioneering a 'third way' constitutes an important precedent, whatever the judgement on her achievements and failures over the last forty years;

– India has a large pool of committed and competent scientists willing to engage in a mutually educating dialogue with their counterparts in other countries and more particularly, to confront their views with those of fellow scientists from the North.

The problematique of a planetary strategy is very broad and, at the same time, bewildering. A Martian technocrat disembarking on our planet, using global statistics would most certainly reach a very optimistic conclusion about the prospect facing the inhabitants of the Earthship.

Thanks to the progress of science and technology already achieved, the age of plenty is within sight. The basic needs of all the humans can be easily satisfied with a reduced burden of work so as to free peoples' time for the cultural, spiritual and playful activities more congenial to the uniqueness of the human species. Although serious uncertainties remain as to the environmental impact of some technologies in use and of excessive fuel energy building, alternative solutions could be worked out by scientists and easily implemented.

Yet, the reality is poles apart from this rosy picture. The world is engulfed by a deep social crisis, compounded by environmental degradation. Its causes are multiple:

– the inequalities built in the working of the economic systems, both within nations and between nations, leading to the twin processes of excessive accumulation of resources in the hands of a minority and of deprivation of the majority; environmental disruption occurs at both ends of the spectrum. The affluent minority with its present lifestyles indulges in over consumption of scarce non-renewable resources while the deprived majority, in order to survive, overtakes the life-supporting systems to which it has an insufficient access;

– the terribly wasteful and environmentally careless patterns of resource-use: the continuing potlatch represented by the piling up of armaments, the exceedingly high operational and transaction costs of the socio-economic and political systems;[3] the paroxysm of 'creative destructiveness' of the productive capacities prompted by an ill-conceived search for competitiveness, the accelerated obsolescence built into equipment and the so-called 'durable' (sic) consumer goods;

– the inadequate priorities of technological research biased towards solvable demand and not towards the satisfaction of basic needs;

– above all, the worst form of irreversible loss represented by the wasting of human lives of all those deprived of their right to work, to earn a decent livelihood and to unfold the potential present in every human being; in modern societies the poor become increasingly useless; alienation and exclusion take the place of exploitation.

Thus, the roots of the social and environmental crisis do not lie in the scarcity of resources. Nor, contrary to a widespread fallacy, in the population explosion. The non-consumers cannot be blamed for over consumption of fossil energy and other resources. Of course, the demographic transition is desirable, as exponential growth of human population on a finite planet cannot be sustained for ever.

But, as pointed out by several contributors to *The Inevitable Billion Plus*, it is not sterilization or contraceptive technology that brings down the rate of population growth but basic economic and social transition. For the 750 million uneducated and poor Indians the argument that a small family is a happy family does not sound

---

[3] Various concepts have been put forward to interpret these costs. Marx spoke of *faux frais* in capitalist production, Georges Bataille of *la part maudite*. For a pioneering study of the costs of private enterprise, see Kapp, K. W. (1971).

convincing. The causal link between population growth and poverty works both ways and to break the vicious circle between the two, eradication of poverty and upgrading of social conditions are the first priority.

An important feature of the present crisis is that it affects, albeit in different forms and with unequal intensity, all the three groups of countries: the late peripheral capitalist countries of the South, the so-called countries in transition from the collapsed 'real socialism' to market-dominated economies and, last but not the least, the industrialized countries of the North plagued by structural unemployment brought about by jobless growth and by a diversion of resources from real economy to the great financial casino.

By far the most spectacular event has been the sudden collapse of the Soviet Union and the discrediting of the centrally planned command economy, paradoxically at a moment when it could theoretically rely on the technical support of powerful computers. The countries of the East are confronted by the daunting task of simultaneously carrying out a structural adjustment, a profound restructuring of the economy and a complete overhaul of economic and political institutions, while facing the prospect of mass unemployment and dealing with a particularly severe environmental crisis, for which they are not prepared.

Yet, their predicament and the failure of their socio-economic system do not constitute a proof *a contrario* of the excellence of capitalism. It is enough to look at the exceedingly high political, social and environmental price paid for the advances in average economic growth and several other indicators by the countries of the Third World, to realize that a sharp departure from the present trends is called for, if the objective is sustainable development, as defined above, achieved through a democratic regulation of mixed economies.

Even more significantly, the welfare states in Western and Northern Europe—a symbol of civilized and socially responsive capitalism—are showing signs of exhaustion, unable to resist the combined pressure of low rates of growth and of a labour-displacing technical progress.[4] The welfare systems have worked

---

[4] During the decade of the sixties world economy grew at the rate of 5 per cent, in the seventies 3.6, in the eighties 2.8 and in the first half of the

well, so long as they were not being put under too much strain of excessive contribution in conditions of rapid growth and almost full employment. But now, when the need for social protection is most pressing, they are crumbling under their cost, not to speak of the fact that mere putting of the unemployed on the dole does not shelter them from social exclusion and loss of dignity[5]; work in our societies still has a major socializing function.

Social exclusion, spatial segregation, ethnic tensions and dualization of the economies—themes once reserved to the discussion of peripheral societies—have acquired a universal pertinence. A severe deficit of economic and social democracy has become a common challenge of the South, East and the North alike with no easy solutions at sight.

More and more, the international configuration acts more as an obstacle than a facilitator. The world economy has gone through a structural transformation brought about by three 'decouplings'[6] (Peter Drucker): the divorce between the growth of output and the creation of working opportunities, the gap between the GNP and the volume of raw materials and commodities required to produce it and, last but not the least, the loosening of the link between the real economy and the financial speculative sphere expanding in a totally uncontrolled way.

Rising productivity is, of course, welcome if properly managed in terms of equitable sharing of the socially required work and of

---

nineties just 2 per cent. 'In two decades capitalism lost 60 per cent of its momentum' (Thurow, L. 1996a). The United States had an average rate of annual GDP growth of 3.4 per cent from 1870 to 1973 and only 2.3 per cent between 1973 and 1993. The output per man hour (productivity) rose at an annual average between 2 and 2.5 per cent from 1950 to 1970, it exceeded 2.5 per cent from 1948 to 1973, then fell to below 1 per cent from 1973 to 1993 (Madrick, J. 1995). The correlation between the rise of neoliberalism and the slowing of the world economy deserves a close scrutiny. Even by its own standards, the 'survival of the fittest capitalism' which dominates the scene today is unable to assert its superiority (Thurow, L. 1996b).

[5] Already in the seventies, the limits of the Welfare State and the impending crisis were perfectly discernible (see Sachs, I., 1982). The Secretariat for Future Studies existing then in Sweden was the focal point for the search of alternative forms of care in society. For a recent summing up of this question see Balbo, L. (1994).

[6] See Drucker, P. (1986).

the product obtained. But this is not the case at present. The pricing of commodities requires international agreement and stabilization schemes which 40 years of discussions have failed to yield. The North–South impasse continues unabated. Absence of controls on the global financial markets, capable of curbing speculation which attracts resources to the detriment of productive investment, constitutes the basic weakness of the Bretton Woods institutions. The IMF does not stand up to its original purpose, preferring instead to play the role of the guardian of monetarian orthodoxy, imposing on developing countries deflation, devaluation and de-regulation irrespective of the prevailing conditions and of the social costs incurred.

Low rates of growth and unemployment sharpen the struggle for markets. Competitiveness is being sought by all means, without distinction between its legitimate and spurious sources, such as depressed wages, severe underpricing of energy and raw materials, and predatory exploitation of natural resources.[7] Left to the free interplay of market forces, enterprises externalize social and environmental costs of production, playing havoc with the rules of social equity and ecological prudence. That is why redefining of the regulatory role of the States and of binding rules of the game on the international scene is urgently called for.

On the one hand, it is necessary to outline need-oriented eco-development strategies, i.e. to make sure that the economic system will be able to produce all the goods and services required to meet the basic needs of the world population without further environmental disruption. The concept of basic needs is understood in its 'strong' version (Ben Wisner): it is up to the populations concerned and not to technocrats using abstract norms to define them in their concrete diversity, while at the same time deploying their resource-fulness by identifying in each ecosystem—be it rural or urban—the latent, underutilized or misused resources to be tapped and/or redirected. Eco-development strategies ought to be ecosystem, culture and site-specific. That is why greater local autonomy and meaningful peoples' participation are required, which should not be misundestood, however, as a way of shunning the responsibility of the central States and of the international system.

---

[7] For a *mise en garde* against the transformation of competitiveness into an all-pervasive ideology, see Group of Lisbon, The (1993).

On the other hand, in order to correspond a solvable demand to the production of satisfactors of basic needs, eco-development strategies ought to pay special attention to the creation of opportunities to work and earn a decent wage and/or to self-produce the livelihood. Employment cannot be treated as merely resultant from the rate of economic growth. Fine-tuned employment policies are called for, for exploring the job opportunities in the following areas:

- resources and energy conservation and recycling, as well as better maintenance of the existing stock of equipment, housing and infrastructure;
- the prospect for a highly productive small-scale agriculture made possible by the second, biology-based, green-revolution;
- the scope for expanding the biomass uses for energy and industrial purposes;
- the potential for rural non-agricultural employment in decentralized industries based on flexible specialization;
- the need for expanded public works in order to improve the systemic competitiveness of national and regional economics through better infrastructure.
- the expansion of social services by means of highly labour-intensive delivery systems.

An active policy of employment creation and productive insertion constitutes the most effective way of addressing the widespread phenomena of social exclusion.

Special attention should be paid to the first priority listed above, insofar as it represents a clear case of a positive-sum game, in which socio-economic and environmental gains go hand in hand, the more so that many jobs created in the realm of resource conservation might pay for themselves through the saving of resources achieved in this way. For obvious reasons, eco-development strategies should concentrate as much as possible on such 'win-win' opportunities which have been rather neglected till today.

References

Balbo, L. (1994), 'From Welfare States to Caring Society', Paper Prepared for the International Conference on Public Policies, Peoples' Actions and Social Development, Bologna 2–3 December.

Drucker, P. (1986), 'The Changed World Economy', *Foreign Affairs*, pp. 768–91.

Gowariker, V. (ed.) (1986), *The Inevitable Billion Plus*, Vichar Dhara Publications, Pune.

Group of Lisbon, The (R. Petrella et al.) (1993), *Limits to Competition*, Gulbenkian Foundation, Lisbon.

Madrick, J. (1995), *The End of Affluence—The Causes and Consequences of America's Economic Dilemma*, Random House, New York.

Kapp, K. W. (1971), *The Social Costs of Private Enterprise*, Schocken Books, New York.

Sachs, I. (1982), 'The Crisis of the Welfare State and Exercise of Social Rights to Development', *International Social Science Journal*, vol. XXXIV, no. 1, Paris.

———— (1993), *Transition Strategies towards the 21st Century*, Interest Publications for Research and Information System for the Non-Aligned and Other Developing Countries.

———— (1994), (in collaboration with V. Gowariker), 'Redefining the Good Society: A North–South Dialogue on Challenges of 21st Century', *Economic and Political Weekly*, 4 June, pp. 1383–5.

Thurow, L. (1996a), *The Future of Capitalism—How Today's Economic Forces Shape.*

———— (1996b), 'The Crusade That's Killing Prosperity', *The American Prospect*, March–April.

Name Index

Subject Index